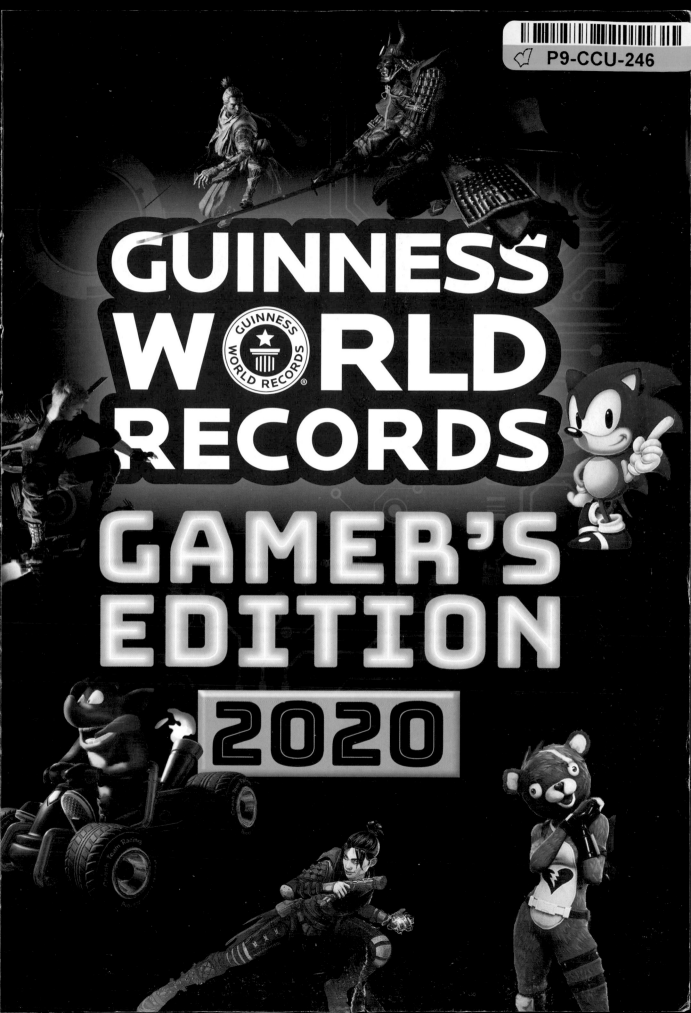

P9-CCU-246

GUINNESS WORLD RECORDS

GUINNESS
WORLD RECORDS®

GAMER'S EDITION

2020

© 2019 GUINNESS WORLD RECORDS LIMITED

No part of this book may be reproduced or transmitted in any form or by any means, electronic, chemical, mechanical, including photography, or used in any information storage or retrieval system without a licence or other permission in writing from the copyright owners.

British Library Cataloguing-in-Publication Data: a catalogue record for this book is available from the British Library.

UK: 978-1-912286-82-9
US: 978-1-912286-85-0
US: 978-1-912286-84-3

Check the official website at guinnessworldrecords.com/gamers for more record-breaking gamers.

ACCREDITATION:
Guinness World Records Limited has a very thorough accreditation system for records verification. However, while every effort is made to ensure accuracy, Guinness World Records Limited cannot be held responsible for any errors contained in this work. Feedback from our readers on any point of accuracy is always welcomed.

Guinness World Records Limited does not claim to own any right, title or interest in the trademarks of others reproduced in this book.

© 2019 Guinness World Records Limited, a Jim Pattison Group company

Records are made to be broken – indeed it is the one of the key criteria for a record category. So, if you find a record that you can beat, tell us about it by making a record claim on our website.

Guinness World Records Limited uses both metric and imperial units. Where a specific date is given, the exchange rate is calculated according to the currency values that were in operation at the time. Where only a year date is given, the exchange rate is calculated from 31 Dec of that year. "One billion" is taken to mean one thousand million.

Appropriate advice should always be taken when attempting to break or set records. Participants undertake records entirely at their own risk. Guinness World Records Limited has complete discretion over whether or not to include any particular record attempts in any of its publications. Being a Guinness World Records record-holder does not guarantee you a place in any *Guinness World Records* publication.

OFFICIALLY AMAZING

THE JIM PATTISON GROUP

GAMER'S EDITION

Gaming Editor
Mike Plant

Layout Editor
Chris Bryans

Editor-in-Chief
Craig Glenday

Senior Editor
Adam Millward

Editor
Ben Hollingum

Proofreading & fact-checking
Tom Beckerlegge, Rob Dimery, Stace Harman,
John Robertson, Matt White

Head of Publishing & Book Production
Jane Boatfield

Head of Pictures & Design
Fran Morales

Picture Researcher
Paul McConnell

Design
Billy Waqar

Artworker
Andrew Sloan

Product Manager
Lucy Acfield

Head of Visual Content
Michael Whitty

Content Producer
Jenny Langridge

Production Director
Patricia Magill

Production Coordinator
Thomas McCurdy

Production Consultants
Roger Hawkins, Florian Seyfert, Tobias Wrona

Reprographics
Res Kahraman and Honor Flowerday at Born Group

Indexer
Marie Lorimer

Printing & Binding
MOHN Media Mohndruck GmbH, Gütersloh, Germany

GUINNESS WORLD RECORDS

GLOBAL HEADQUARTERS
Global President: Alistair Richards
Professional Services
Alison Ozanne
Category Management: Benjamin Backhouse, Jason Fernandes, Sheila Mella Suárez, Will Munford, Shane Murphy, Luke Wakeham
Finance: Tobi Amusan, Jusna Begum, Elizabeth Bishop, Jess Blake, Yusuf Gafar, Lisa Gibbs, Kimberley Jones, Nhan Nguyen, Sutharsan Ramachandran, Jamie Sheppard, Scott Shore, Andrew Wood
HR & Office Management: Jackie Angus, Alexandra Ledin, Farrella Ryan-Coker, Monika Tilani
IT: Céline Bacon, Ashleigh Bair, John Cvitanovic, Diogo Gomes, Rob Howe, Benjamin Mclean, Cenk Selim, Alpha Serrant-Defoe
Legal: Catherine Loughran, Raymond Marshall, Kaori Minami, Mehreen Moghul

Brand Strategy, Content & Product, Creative
Sam Fay, Katie Forde, Paul O'Neill
Brand Partnerships: Juliet Dawson
Design: Edward Dillon, Alisa Zaytseva
Digital: Veronica Irons, Alex Waldu
Product Marketing: Lucy Acfield, Rebecca Lam, Emily Osborn, Mawa Rodriguez, Louise Toms
Visual Content: Sam Birch-Machin, Karen Gilchrist, Jenny Langridge, Matthew Musson, Joseph O'Neil, Catherine Pearce, Alan Pixsley, Jonathan Whitton, Michael Whitty
Website & Social Content: David Stubbings, Dan Thorne

EMEA & APAC
Nadine Causey
Brand & Content
Marketing & PR: Nicholas Brookes, Lauren Cochrane, Jessica Dawes, Imelda Ekpo, Amber-Georgina Gill, Lauren Johns, Doug Male, Connie Suggitt
Publishing Sales: Caroline Lake, Helene Navarre, Joel Smith
Records Management: Lewis Blakeman, Adam Brown, Tara El Kashef, Daniel Kidane, Mark McKinley

Consultancy - UKROW
Neil Foster
Client Account Services: Sonia Chadha-Nihal, Fay Edwards, Samuel Evanson, Andrew Fanning, William Hume-Humphreys, Soma Huy, Irina Nohailic, Sam Prosser, Nikhil Shukla, Sadie Smith
Event Production: Fiona Gruchy-Craven, Danny Hickson
Marketing & PR: Lisa Lambert, Iliyan Stoychev, Amanda Tang
Records Management: Matilda Hagne, Paul Hillman, Christopher Lynch, Maria Raggi

Consultancy – MENA
Talal Omar
Client Account Services: Naser Batat, Mohammad Kiswani, Kamel Yassin
HR & Office Management: Monisha Bimal
Marketing & PR: Aya Ali, Leila Issa
Records Management: Hoda Khachab, Samer Khallouf

EAST ASIA
Marco Frigatti
China
Client Account Services: Blythe Fitzwilliam, Catherine Gao, Chloe Liu, Tina Ran, Amelia Wang, Elaine Wang, Ivy Wang, Jin Yu, Jacky Yuan
HR & Office Management: Tina Shi, Crystal Xu
Legal: Paul Nightingale, Jiayi Teng
Marketing & PR: Tracy Cui, Karen Pan, Vanessa Tao, Angela Wu, Echo Zhan, Naomi Zhang, Yvonne Zhang, Delling Zhao, Emily Zeng
Records Management: Fay Jiang, Ted Li, Reggy Lu, Charles Wharton, Winnie Zhang, Alicia Zhao
Japan
Erika Ogawa
Client Account Services: Blythe Fitzwilliam, Wei Liang, Takuro Maruyama, Yuki Morishita, Yumiko Nakagawa, Masamichi Yazaki
HR & Office Management: Emiko Yamamoto
Marketing & PR: Kazami Kamioka, Vihag Kulshrestha, Aya McMillan, Momoko Satou, Masakazu Senda, Yumi Uota, Eri Yuhira

Records Management: Aki Ichikawa, Kaoru Ishikawa, Momoko Omori, Koma Satoh, Lala Teranishi, Yuki Uebo

AMERICAS
Alistair Richards
North America
Client Account Services: Alex Angert, Mackenzie Berry, David Canela, Danielle Levy, Nicole Pando, Kimberly Partrick, Michelle Santucci
HR & Office Management: Vincent Acevedo, Jennifer Olson
Marketing, PR & Publishing Sales: Valerie Esposito, Lauren Festa, Michael Furnari, Rachel Gluck, Elizabeth Montoya, Morganna Nickoff, Rachel Silver, Kristen Stephenson, Sonja Valenta
Records Management: Spencer Cammarano, Christine Fernandez, Hannah Ortman, Callie Smith, Claire Stephens, Kaitlin Vesper
Latin America
Carlos Martinez
Client Account Services: Carolina Guanabara-Hall, Ralph Hannah, Jaime Rodriguez
Marketing & PR: Laura Angel, Alice Marie Pagán-Sánchez
Records Management: Raquel Assis, Jaime Oquendo

OFFICIAL ADJUDICATORS
Camila Borenstain, Joanne Brent, Jack Brockbank, Sarah Casson, Dong Cheng, Christina Conlon, Swapnil Dangarikar, Casey DeSantis, Brittany Dunn, Michael Empric, Pete Fairbairn, Victor Fenes, Fumika Fujibuchi, Ahmed Gabr, John Garland, Şeyda Subaşı Gemici, Andy Glass, Sofia Greenacre, Iris Hou, Rei Iwashita, Louis Jelinek, Kazuyoshi Kirimura, Mariko Koike, Lena Kuhlmann, Maggie Luo, Solvej Malouf, Mike Marcotte, Mai McMillan, Rishi Nath, Chika Onaka, Anna Orford, Douglas Palau, Kellie Parise, Pravin Patel, Justin Patterson, Glenn Pollard, Natalia Ramirez, Stephanie Randall, Cassie Ren, Philip Robertson, Paulina Sapinska, Tomomi Sekioka, Hiroaki Shino, Lucia Sinigagliesi, Brian Sobel, Kevin Southam, Richard Stenning, Carlos Tapia, Lorenzo Veltri, Xiong Wen, Peter Yang

INTRO

Hello, readers – it's Ali-A here!

It's absolutely fantastic to be back in the *GWR Gamer's Edition* for 2020 – a year that feels like a landmark in itself. Just think, the last time I wrote an introduction – in 2016 for the 2017 *Gamer's Edition* – Nintendo had yet to announce the Switch and there was no such thing as *Fortnite*!

What a difference a few years make. The one thing that you can always depend on is that gamers will keep on pushing the boundaries to set more and more incredible records. The other thing you can guarantee is that my favourite, Super Mario (pp.20–21), will save the Mushroom Kingdom from Bowser, Link (pp.68–69) will free Hyrule and Kratos (pp.78–79) will get really angry. Which is why I'm so excited to see that this year's book has pages dedicated to those three characters – and lots more besides.

But as I've already mentioned, the game that's simply taken the industry by storm is, of course, *Fortnite*! As those of you who follow me online will know, I absolutely love playing *Fortnite* and I'm always thrilled to read about it, too. That's why I'm so happy to see that the *Gamer's Edition* has an entire chapter (pp.50–63) dedicated to Epic Games' brilliant battle royale.

My favourite record in that chapter, and possibly the entire book, has to be that of "RockyNoHands" (pp.60–61), an American gamer who had a really bad accident that meant he was paralysed. Despite that, he was able to teach himself how to play *Fortnite* – and lots of other games – by just using his mouth. Wow! His bravery and skill just leave me speechless. Another record that caught my eye was that of "HighDistortion" (pp.50–51), as he reached 100,000 eliminations in *Fortnite* before anyone else!

I don't think it matters who you are, or what game you play – you can always strive to be the best and have a go at breaking a record! As I know well, it's a great feeling to set a new Guinness World Records title. Here's hoping that in years to come I'll be reading about a record that you've set in the *Gamer's Edition!*

I'll see you online!

Ali-A

Ali-A

3

And you thought *your* games collection was big!
The **largest collection of videogames** consists of 20,139 items and was achieved by Antonio Romero Monteiro (USA) in Richmond, Texas, USA, on 2 Feb 2019. The hoard includes complete North American sets of games for the Genesis, PS2, PS3, PSP, PS Vita, Xbox, Xbox 360, SNES, GameCube, Wii and Wii U. Of Monteiro's rarer items, he owns every game for the Nintendo 64DD (the Japan-only disk-drive peripheral for the N64) and *CJ Elephant Fugitive* (Codemasters, 1994) – a seldom-seen Game Gear title.

Of all the titles in his collection, Monteiro's favourite is Konami's *Super Castlevania IV* (1991) for the Super NES. "This is by far my most beloved game," he told us. "I love this game. I think it's a masterpiece."

CONTENTS

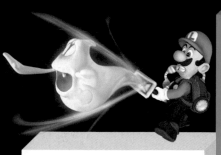

EDITOR'S LETTER

Welcome one and all to the *Guinness World Records Gamer's Edition 2020*. Let me start by asking you a question: who is your favourite gaming character? Maybe Mario? Perhaps Sonic? What about Spider-Man, Pikachu, Link, Cloud, Snake, Kratos, Samus or Lara Croft? If you answered any of the above you're in luck, but even if you didn't, there's every chance that your most-loved character will be featured in this book.

That's because *Gamer's Edition 2020* is themed around the biggest stars of the videogame world. Every page is bursting with records, facts and trivia about our heroes, whether they're old hands like Mario, or relative newcomers such as *Red Dead 2*'s Arthur Morgan (pp.84–85) or the Apex Legends (pp.106–07). But don't think that we've forgotten about real-life record holders.

REAL-LIFE VIDEOGAME GREATS

You'll find that your favourite Twitch streamers, YouTubers, e-sports pros, speed-runners and fighting-game champions are all here, too.

And so is a very special guest whose voice is one of the most famous in the world – Charles Martinet. Charles has provided the voice of Mario since the mid-1990s, and I was lucky enough to meet him when he popped in for a visit at GWR's HQ in London, UK. See pp.20–21 for more on how he became the person with the **most videogame voice-over performances as the same character**!

This year's special chapter is about a game that almost everyone on the planet will have heard of by now: *Fortnite*. Epic's title is nothing short of a phenomenon, so we've created 14 pages covering everything from the best players and the rarest skins to a history of the game's seasons. You could even "build" yourself into the next *Gamer's Edition* by getting inventive in *Fortnite*'s Creative Mode – see pp.62–63.

NEW DIRECTIONS FOR GWR AND GAMING

Finally, it's only fitting that I use this introduction to let our readers know about two important pieces of news that I'm very proud of. The first is our new partnership with Speedrun.com, which will allow speed-runners to apply directly for Guinness World Record titles. Turn to pp.142–43 to find out more about how you can apply and what you need to do to have a go at attempting a record.

The other thing I must mention is the *GWR Gamer's Podcast*. Every two weeks, I get together with the podcast's other regulars to talk about the latest games, the biggest news and the most interesting gaming records. Find the latest episode at: www.guinnessworldrecords.com/gamers.

I look forward to hearing your thoughts on the book, and I hope you have as much fun reading it as we had writing it! All that's left for me to do is thank everyone here who contributes to the book and, of course, thank all of you for reading it!

May you never need a "Continue",

Mike Plant
Editor,
GWR Gamer's Edition

YEAR IN GAMING PART 1

From treasure hunts and crazy stunts to trending memes and gold-medal events, you'll see that plenty has happened in the world of gaming this year. And the stories here are just for starters – turn over the page for Part 2...

A real-life treasure hunt

Destiny 2 is known for its in-game loot, but a strange symbol in Al Rasputin's bunker led players on a real treasure hunt that ended in New York state, USA. On 12 May, "I_love_science" was rewarded with an ornate spear, gold coin and a note from the developer of the "Warmind" DLC.

Going for gold

On 14 May, it was announced that a select few competitive videogames would be included in the 2018 Asian Games – a sporting event held every four years. Riot Games' *League of Legends* (2009) was one of those titles chosen, with China (above) emerging victorious on 29 Aug.

Magnificent trailer; moderate game

As of 22 Feb 2019, the **most watched game trailer to debut at E3 2018** was that of *Fallout 76* (Bethesda), with 34,363,981 views. But that's where the good news ends, as, upon its 2018 release, the game received widespread criticism.

"Piano Man" strikes the right chord

At a DreamHack event in Austin, Texas, USA, "Can EC Greg" (CAN) played *Dragon Ball FighterZ* with... a piano keyboard! His unusual performance was no gimmick – the gamer avoided making any wrong notes and his nimble fingers took him to a place in the event's last eight. It's no surprise that his new nickname of "Piano Man" has stuck.

London Spitfire shoot down rivals to reign as *Overwatch* overlords

The London Spitfire team became the **first champions of the *Overwatch* League Grand Finals**, despite not being favoured by many to make it through the play-offs. At the Barclays Center in Brooklyn, New York, USA, the UK-based franchise won 2–0 overall, defeating Philadelphia Fusion 3–1 on 27 Jul and then 3–0 the following day. Victory brought the team, made up of South Korean players, the $1,000,000 (£762,920) first prize. Turn to pp.168–69 for more records from the *Overwatch* League's first season.

No rest at insomnia63

As gamers descended on Birmingham, UK, for insomnia63, Guinness World Records was on hand to encourage attendees to write themselves into history. Over four days, 14 records were set, including one by Alex Newby (UK, above), who achieved the **fastest time to build a three-storey wooden fort in _Fortnite's_ Playground mode**, taking 50.12 sec. Do you want to try a _Fortnite_ Creative mode challenge yourself? Turn to pp.62–63...

EarthBound no longer

What would you choose if given the chance to send an object 100,000 ft (30,480 m) up to the edge of space? The chances are it wouldn't be a game that was released way before you were born. Teenager Ronnie Doyle did just that, though, deciding to launch the classic Super Nintendo RPG _EarthBound_ (1994) – clearly with a nod to irony, given the game's title. Thankfully, his cartridge returned from its trip in a helium balloon still in good working order, with its precious save files intact.

The sad story of Telltale Games

California-based games developer Telltale scored its biggest hit in 2012 with _The Walking Dead_. Unfortunately, on 21 Sep, it, too, joined the ranks of the deceased. A skeleton crew was kept on, but the doors closed for good in November. At least we'll always have the memories of playing through some of gaming's best narrative adventures, including _The Wolf Among Us_ (2013) and _Tales from the Borderlands_ (2014).

Even Mario looks lost for words

What do you get if you cross Bowser with Princess Peach? The answer is Bowsette (above right). Artist "ayyk92" shared their creation on 29 Sep. Variations on the meme spiralled out of control on social media, though Nintendo has squashed any hopes we had for Bowsette becoming canon.

What's in a name?

It's been the complaint of many a PlayStation owner that they've been unable to change their PSN gamertags. On 10 Oct, Sony corrected the long-standing oversight by confirming it would be possible to change your PSN name from early 2019. Time to put that embarrassing gamertag behind you!

Teenager is perfect fit as new _Tetris_ king

With seven world titles, Jonas Neubauer (USA, far right) was the _Tetris_ king. But on 21 Oct he was unseated by Joseph Saelee (USA, right), who became the **youngest _Tetris_ world champion** at the Classic Tetris World Championship in Portland, Oregon, USA. At just 16 years old, Saelee's age drew media attention, but then so did his "hypertapping" technique. Throughout the tournament, Saelee furiously tapped down on his NES controller's D-pad – rather than simply holding it – to make his bricks fall faster than those of his rivals.

YEAR IN GAMING PART 2

A busy beginning to our gaming year gave way to an even busier second half. Among the announcements and the controversies was a Google press conference that might have revealed how the way we play games will change for ever...

NOV 2018

Diabolical *Diablo*

Hype is part and parcel of gaming, but there has to be substance too. Blizzard learned this to its cost when it released a trailer for *Diablo Immortal* on 2 Nov. Fans were hoping for news of *Diablo IV* – not a mobile version of their beloved franchise. The trailer suffered the fans' wrath, with negative comments pouring in and dislikes hitting 738,000 as of 29 Mar 2019 (compared to just 28,000 likes).

Sony opts out of E3

News broke on 15 Nov that Sony would be conspicuous by its absence at E3 in Jun 2019. A Sony statement said that the publisher was seeking other ways to engage with gamers, and it duly followed up on the promise by debuting its PlayStation State of Play gaming update on YouTube in Mar 2019.

DEC 2018

Stormy time for e-sports pros

In a not-great couple of months for Blizzard, the cancellation of the *Heroes of the Storm* Global Championship Grand Finals went down badly with e-sports pros. Unsurprising, given that a pot of $1 m (£769,678) had been up for grabs at 2018's event.

Shape of things to come?

When a poster was released on 10 Dec for Sonic's Nov 2019 movie, even the speedster hedgehog struggled to keep pace with reactions on social media. Influencers were abuzz at the sight of the hedgehog's outsized legs and human-like proportions. Then there was the question of Sonic's fur – something you don't see very much of on a real hedgehog, which has rather more in the way of quills...

2018: A HUGE YEAR IN GAMING

The verdict on the gaming industry after a successful 2018 was that it's in the rudest of health. In the US, the industry generated a staggering $43.4 bn (£34.1 bn), as both hardware and software sales took huge steps in the right direction. The market was similarly buoyant across the Atlantic. Videogame sales topped $7.2 bn (£5.6 bn) in the UK, meaning that gaming commanded a larger share of the entertainment market than music and movies combined! *Red Dead Redemption 2* (13.94 million units sold), *Marvel's Spider-Man* (8.76 million) and *God of War* (6.15 million) were all huge hits, while *Fortnite* and *Apex Legends* were online success stories.

The tooth about sharks and games

What was the link between a classic arcade game of the 1980s and an extinct shark that lived over 65 million years ago? The answer lay in an amazing discovery made by experts at North Carolina State University. Apparently, the tiny teeth belonging to a previously unknown species of small shark, living in what is now South Dakota, USA, resembled the player-controlled starfighter in Namco's arcade game *Galaga* (1981). Scientists named the shark appropriately, calling it *Galagadon nordquistae* (an artist's impression of the shark is right).

At last, Bowser is calling the shots

Bowser has craved power for years and now he's got it – except this is Doug Bowser, Nintendo of America's new boss. In the past, he'd even playfully tied up Mario and Luigi – take a look over his shoulder (above)!

No accounting for taste

The tall, dark and gruesome Waluigi received 1,261,539 Valentine's Day votes, as of 29 Mar 2019, after Nintendo had set up a poll to mark the special February day. Fans of Waluigi hope that doing what they can to say how much they love the anti-Luigi might nudge Nintendo into finally making a game starring Wario's partner in crime!

The future of gaming?

On 19 Mar, Google took to the stage at the Game Developers Conference in San Francisco, USA, to announce Stadia. The videogame-streaming service can stream games (without having to install a thing) to any device with the Chrome browser. But Google stopped short of announcing how much the service would cost. Expect all to be revealed sometime in late 2019.

Magic for Muggles

Revealed on 11 Mar, *Harry Potter: Wizards Unite* will apply the *Pokémon GO* formula to the wizarding world. Niantic's augmented-reality mobile game lets players cast spells and fight Death Eaters in the real world.

Nintendo gets virtual

On 12 Apr, the Nintendo Labo: VR Kit turned the Switch into a set of VR goggles, much like Google Daydream does for Android phones. Even better for Switch owners, the VR Kit took advantage of updates to *The Legend of Zelda: Breath of the Wild* and *Super Mario Odyssey* (both 2017) to add VR elements to the pair of Nintendo games.

Beans spilled on PS5

On 16 Apr, PlayStation's Mark Cerny – the PS4's lead system architect – revealed the first details of the PS5 in an interview with *Wired*. He confirmed that it will be backwards-compatible with PS4 titles and showed how its solid-state drive will dramatically cut loading times.

AWARDS ROUND-UP

Kratos is feared far and wide, but thanks to his 2018 adventure, the God of War is now also being worshipped at the major videogame awards ceremonies. His latest outing picked up five of the six "best game" gongs – only missing out at the Golden Joystick Awards.

36th Golden Joystick Awards
16 Nov 2018, London, UK

AWARD	WINNER
ULTIMATE GAME OF THE YEAR	Fortnite Battle Royale
Best storytelling	God of War
Best visual design	God of War
Best audio	God of War
Best performer	Bryan Dechart (as Connor in Detroit: Become Human)
Best indie game	Dead Cells
Best cooperative game	Monster Hunter World
Studio of the year	SIE Santa Monica Studio
Best VR game	The Elder Scrolls V: Skyrim VR
e-sports game of the year	Overwatch
Best streamer/broadcaster	Bryan Dechart/Amelia Rose Blaire
Mobile game of the year	PLAYERUNKNOWN'S BATTLEGROUNDS
Lifetime achievement	Hidetaka Miyazaki
Best competitive game	Fortnite Battle Royale
Most-wanted award	Cyberpunk 2077 (CD Projekt Red)
Outstanding contribution	Xbox Adaptive Controller

Game Developers Choice Awards
20 Mar 2019, San Francisco, USA

AWARD	WINNER
GAME OF THE YEAR	God of War
Best audio	Celeste
Best debut	Mountains (for Florence)
Best design	Into the Breach
Innovation award	Nintendo Labo
Best narrative	Return of the Obra Dinn
Best technology	Red Dead Redemption 2
Best visual art	Gris
Best VR/AR game	Beat Saber
Lifetime achievement	Amy Hennig

The Game Awards 2018
6 Dec 2018, Los Angeles, USA

AWARD	WINNER
GAME OF THE YEAR	God of War
Best game direction	God of War
Best narrative	Red Dead Redemption 2
Best action game	Dead Cells
Best art direction	Return of the Obra Dinn
Best role-playing game	Monster Hunter World
Best fighting game	Dragon Ball FighterZ
Best family game	Overcooked! 2
Best action/adventure game	God of War
Best score/music	Red Dead Redemption 2
Best audio design	Red Dead Redemption 2
Best performance	Roger Clark (as Arthur Morgan in Red Dead Redemption 2)
Best ongoing game	Fortnite
Games for impact	Celeste
Best VR/AR game	Astro Bot Rescue Mission
Best strategy game	Into the Breach
Best sports/racing game	Forza Horizon 4
Best multiplayer game	Fortnite
Best independent game	Celeste
Best debut indie game	The Messenger
Best e-sports game	Overwatch
Best mobile game	Florence
Best student game	Combat 2018

SXSW Gaming Awards
16 Mar 2019, Austin, USA

AWARD	WINNER
GAME OF THE YEAR	God of War
Excellence in visual achievement	God of War
Excellence in technical achievement	Red Dead Redemption 2
Excellence in SFX	Red Dead Redemption 2
Excellence in narrative	Detroit: Become Human
Excellence in multiplayer	Fortnite
Excellence in musical score	Tetris Effect
Excellence in gameplay	Super Smash Bros. Ultimate
Excellence in design	God of War
Excellence in convergence	Marvel's Spider-Man
Excellence in animation	Marvel's Spider-Man
Excellence in art	Octopath Traveler
Most promising new intellectual property	Beat Saber
Most fulfilling community-funded game	CrossCode
Matthew Crump cultural innovation award	Celeste
Trending game of the year	Red Dead Redemption 2
Most promising new e-sports game	Fortnite
VR game of the year	Beat Saber
Most evolved game	No Man's Sky NEXT
Mobile game of the year	Donut County

British Academy Games Awards (BAFTA)
4 Apr 2019, London, UK

AWARD	WINNER
BEST GAME	God of War
Artistic achievement	Return of the Obra Dinn
Audio achievement	God of War
British game	Forza Horizon 4
Debut game	Yoku's Island Express
Evolving game	Fortnite Battle Royale
Family	Nintendo Labo
Game beyond entertainment	My Child Lebensborn
Game design	Return of the Obra Dinn
Game innovation	Nintendo Labo
Mobile game	Florence
Multiplayer	A Way Out
Music	God of War
Narrative	God of War
Original property	Into the Breach
Performer	Jeremy Davies (as The Stranger in God of War)

DICE 22nd Annual Awards
14 Feb 2019, Las Vegas, USA

AWARD	WINNER
GAME OF THE YEAR	God of War
Action game of the year	Celeste
Adventure game of the year	God of War
Family game of the year	Unravel Two
Fighting game of the year	Super Smash Bros. Ultimate
Immersive reality game of the year	Beat Saber
Portable game of the year	Florence
Outstanding achievement for an independent game	Celeste
Outstanding achievement in animation	Marvel's Spider-Man
Outstanding achievement in character	Kratos (God of War)
Outstanding achievement in game design	God of War
Outstanding achievement in online gameplay	Fortnite
Outstanding achievement in original music composition	God of War
Outstanding achievement in sound design	God of War
Outstanding achievement in story	God of War
Outstanding technical achievement	Red Dead Redemption 2
Racing game of the year	Forza Horizon 4
Role-playing game of the year	Monster Hunter World
Sports game of the year	Mario Tennis Aces
Strategy/simulation game of the year	Into the Breach

HARDWARE

This time next year, there's every chance that we'll be bringing you the launch details of the PS5 and the next Xbox – not this year, though. Instead, there's news of a truly ground-breaking controller, the end of two PlayStation consoles and the tiniest arcade game ever built...

The importance of inclusivity

Traditionally, gamers with disabilities have had to devise ways of playing games with existing controllers. But the Xbox Adaptive Controller (XAC) – the **first official adaptive controller** – made the technology fit the person, rather than the other way round. Microsoft began development of the device in 2015, eventually releasing it in Sep 2018. The rectangular box includes a series of ports that correspond to the buttons on an Xbox One controller. This allows almost any combination of customized devices and controllers to be hooked up to an Xbox One or PC to meet particular requirements.

Game anytime, anywhere...

In Oct 2018, further details were released about Microsoft's Project xCloud, a service that will give Xbox One gamers the freedom to stream their games to a smartphone or other mobile device. The company denied, though, that this would be part of a shift away from traditional console gaming.

The news arrived just before Google announced its forthcoming Stadia game-streaming service (pp.10–11). With both systems, the question on every gamer's lips was how smooth the streaming would be when used with the typical broadband connection.

A myth no more

In Nov 2018, the National Videogame Museum in Frisco, Texas, USA, unearthed a vintage console long thought to be a myth. The Mini Vectrex was designed to be a portable(ish!) version of the 1980s Vectrex console. The commercial failure of its big brother led to the Mini Vectrex being shelved and (almost) forgotten. When it surfaced, it could still play its built-in shooter *Mine Storm*.

Insert (very small) coin

When Jonathan Charles of Germanton, North Carolina, USA, read about what was the existing record for the **smallest arcade machine**, he decided to break it. His miniature masterpiece, verified on 18 Oct 2018, duly did so. It stands just 66.5 mm (2.61 in) tall – that's close to half the size of the previous record holder (124 mm/4.88 in). As you can see, Jonathan's creation played *Space Invaders*.

ACTUAL SIZE • ACTUAL SIZE • ACTUAL SIZE •

A tale of two consoles

In 2018, we waved goodbye to a pair of Sony consoles whose fortunes in the marketplace couldn't have been more contrasting...

In March, production stopped on the handheld PS Vita. In the years after its release in 2011, the console attracted a following of hardcore enthusiasts, yet the Vita never truly took off. A lack of sales resulted in a lack of new games and vice versa.

The other console retired in 2018 couldn't be more different: the **all-time best-selling console** – the PS2. No new PS2s had been built since 2012, but Sony had continued to repair faults. That came to an end in early September when after-sales support for the console was finally withdrawn, some 19 years 6 months since it debuted in Japan on 4 Mar 2000. Thanks for all the memories, PS2!

At home with Capcom

On 16 Apr 2019, Capcom announced its Capcom Home Arcade, a plug-and-play system featuring 16 classic arcade games. The above image isn't a mock-up, either. The system really is in the shape of the Japanese publisher's logo – albeit with buttons and joysticks poking out. Standout titles include *Final Fight, Ghouls 'n Ghosts, Street Fighter II: Hyper Fighting, Darkstalkers: The Night Warriors* and *Alien vs. Predator*. The last of those is a side-scrolling beat-'em-up that's never been released on a home system before.

How to make a wee Wii for yourself

This pint-sized "PiiWii" crams the circuit boards of the Wii – and a 8.89-cm (3.5-in) display – into a plastic case that measures just 14 cm by 8 cm (5.5 x 3.1 in). To make it, "Shank" (USA) had to cut the Wii's circuit boards down to size and then use wires to connect the various components back together. The finished device even has a built-in sensor bar and can play Wii and GameCube games via a USB stick.

An epic quest for VR

Square Enix's long-running RPG franchise *Dragon Quest* is a phenomenon in Japan, which explains why there was so much excitement when the **first *Dragon Quest* VR game** was revealed in Apr 2018. The arcade-only experience is available to play at Bandai Namco's VR Zone in Shinjuku, Tokyo, Japan. As a warrior, a mage or a priest, players battle Smile Slimes and other iconic monsters from the franchise.

GOLDEN

There are some videogames and characters that only seem to get better with age. Here, we celebrate gaming's rich heritage of classic icons and the vintage titles they star in.

DONKEY KONG

Highest score for the first level of *Donkey Kong*

The current game-leading score for level 1-1 of *Donkey Kong* is 12,600. It was achieved by US expert Jeremy Young and verified by Twin Galaxies on 24 Feb 2018. He was granted one life to complete the stage but could score points by any means, including jumping Kong's barrels and whacking them with a hammer.

PAC-MAN

Fastest time to achieve 10,000 points

It took speedy Canadian player "Remz" just 43.6 sec to break the 10,000-point barrier in *PAC-Man*. The dot-chomping, ghost-busting record was achieved on 18 Mar 2018, using an emulated version of Namco's original 1980 arcade game, and was verified on the same day by Speedrun.

Q*BERT

First "curse word" in a game

Did the cube-hopping Q*bert utter gaming's first expletive in 1982? Well, kind of... In order to avoid censorship, Q*bert's would-be profanity (which appeared in a speech bubble when he lost a life) consisted of the nonsense characters "@!#?@!". It's a good job nobody speaks Q*bertese!

DIG DUG

Most points scored in *Dig Dug*

Donald Hayes (USA) digged and dugged his way to a huge score of 5,147,610 on 23 Apr 2017 while playing Namco's 1982 arcade classic. As verified by Twin Galaxies, his tally beat the previous record – Ken House's (USA) score of 4,446,760 – by 700,850 points.

MS. PAC-MAN

First playable female character in a videogame

Long before Lara Croft and *Metroid*'s Samus, Ms. PAC-Man paved the way for empowered female videogame characters. The *Ms. PAC-Man* coin-op cabinet was released by Bally/Midway in 1982 and quickly became a massive hit.

OLDIES

DUKE NUKEM

Longest development period for a videogame

Living up to its name, *Duke Nukem Forever* took practically for ever to see the light of day. The sequel to 1996's *Duke Nukem 3D* was officially announced on 28 Apr 1997, but it wasn't released until 10 Jun 2011: a total development time of 14 years 43 days!

FROGGER

First board game based on a videogame

Assassin's Creed, *The Witcher* and *BioShock* have all been given board-game makeovers. But the first videogame-to-board-game conversion was Konami's *Frogger*. Milton Bradley (MB Games) released its surprisingly faithful dice-rolling rendition in 1981.

SPACE INVADERS

Highest score on the original arcade *Space Invaders*

Jon Tannahill (AUS) set a new *Space Invaders* high score of 218,870 points on 13 Jan 2018, as verified by Twin Galaxies. Using a 1978 Taito arcade cabinet, he took 3 hr 47 min 56 sec, with the game's score rolling over from 9,990 and back to zero 21 times.

DIRK THE DARING

First games released on every optical disc platform

When Dirk the Daring entered *Dragon's Lair* in 1983, little did he know that his adventure would take him to every kind of optical disc, including LaserDisc, CD, DVD and Blu-ray. He was matched by his spiritual brother Dexter, hero of 1984's *Space Ace*.

BJ BLAZKOWICZ

Most videogame releases across generations of characters

Not only does BJ Blazkowicz appear in 11 *Wolfenstein* games, but it turns out he is also the grandfather of Billy Blaze, the hero of five *Commander Keen* games, and the great-grandfather of the DOOM Slayer (12 games, pp.108–09). This means the Blazkowicz bloodline spans 28 games!

MEGASTARS

Games are full of awesome characters, but only a select few are so famous that even your non-gamer friends and family would recognize them. Here we celebrate the *crème de la crème* of gaming...

MOST VIDEOGAME VOICE-OVER PERFORMANCES AS THE SAME CHARACTER

The release of *Super Smash Bros. Ultimate* for the Switch on 7 Dec 2018 marked the 100th occasion that the USA's Charles Martinet (pictured, far right, with *Gamer's Edition* editor Mike Plant) had provided the voice of Nintendo's iconic character Super Mario.

Charles's game debut was in *Mario's Game Gallery* (aka *Mario's FUNdamentals*) for the PC in 1995. The release was a largely forgettable collection of mini-games, but it was notable for featuring a talking Mario, complete with his famous high-pitched vocals.

COMING UP ▶▶▶

SUPER MARIO

It only takes a beat of *that* iconic music, a glance at those famous red-and-blue overalls or a whisper of "it's-a me" to know that you're looking at a *Super Mario* game. He's gaming's most famous son, Nintendo's "number 1" – and a heck of a hero.

BIG DEBUT

Mario first appeared in *Donkey Kong* in 1981, but was known only as "Jumpman".

Most *Mario Kart 64* non-shortcut course records

As of 22 Aug 2018, German speedster "MR" (aka Matthias Rustemeyer) held 29 of the 32 non-shortcut course records for *Mario Kart 64*. His tally comprises 15 three-lap course record times and 14 fastest individual lap times. His bid to become the first holder of every course record is being closely monitored by *Mario Kart* tracking site www.mkwrs.com.

NEMESIS

Bowser – scourge of the Mushroom Kingdom and perennial abductor of Princess Peach – is also gaming's **most ubiquitous villain**. As of 11 Jan 2019, he'd starred in 132 titles, often prompting Mario's next adventure.

Largest collection of *Super Mario* memorabilia

Japan's Mitsugu Kikai has built up an amazing array of Mario memorabilia. At its last count on 15 Jul 2010, it contained 5,441 unique items, including games, plushies, pins, DVDs and more. Mitsugu estimates his collection has since doubled in size – something we're investigating.

POWER-UP

Mario has utilized some of gaming's most iconic power-ups over the years. Here, we take you on a guide of some of our favourites from his classic games...

Mushroom (1985) *Super Mario Bros.*

Frog Suit (1988) *Super Mario Bros. 3*

Cape Feather (1990) *Super Mario World*

Wing Cap (1996) *Super Mario 64*

Blue Shell (2006) *New Super Mario Bros.*

Most prolific party videogame series

Super Mario Party's arrival on the Switch on 5 Oct 2018 marked the 16th time that Mario and friends have got together to party. First launched in 1998 for the N64, the series progressed to GameCube, Wii, Wii U and Switch, also taking the odd detour to Nintendo's GBA, DS and 3DS handheld consoles.

Fastest time to make Mario shirtless in *Super Mario Odyssey*

Nintendo's creation of a custom *Super Mario Odyssey* costume that puts Mario in just his boxer shorts – so revealing his chest for the first time – has inspired a new Speedrun category. The feat, widely known as the "Nipple%" run, was achieved by the UK's "Timpani" in 9 min 55 sec, as verified on 29 May 2018.

MARIO
00020   WORLD   TIME
                          1-1   365

QUICK FACT: Super Mario was named after Mario Segale (USA), a real-estate developer who was Nintendo's landlord in 1981. Segale sadly passed away in Oct 2018.

BEST-SELLING *SUPER MARIO* GAME

Out of the way *Odyssey*, gangway *Galaxy*, because it's 1985's *Super Mario Bros.* for the NES that's the famous plumber's best-selling game. As of 11 Jan 2019, *Super Mario Bros.* was still out in front of any other *Mario* title, selling 40.24 million copies. It's the second-best-selling physical release of all time, with only *Wii Sports* (2006) performing better, shifting a huge 82.65 million copies.

The NES classic also inspired the **first live-action movie based on a videogame**. *Super Mario Bros.* was distributed by Buena Vista Pictures in 1993 and starred Bob Hoskins as Mario.

Ice Flower (2007)
Super Mario Galaxy

Penguin Suit (2009)
New Super Mario Bros. Wii

Rock Mushroom (2010)
Super Mario Galaxy 2

Super Acorn (2012)
New Super Mario Bros. U

Super Bell (2013)
Super Mario 3D World

Cappy (2017)
Super Mario Odyssey

SNAPSHOT

Jaws gaped, tongues lolled and gamers gasped upon seeing just the title screen – never mind the extraordinary gameplay – of 1996's *Super Mario 64*. Mario's face was realized in full 3D for the first time (left) and could even be contorted using the N64's controller. Nintendo also included a guide to doing just that in the game's manual.

LOVE STORY

LOVE-O-METER

Mario might be saying "*ti amo*" to Princess Peach, but if events in *Super Mario Odyssey* are anything to go by, she's playing very hard to get. Still, Mario's repeated rescues of her have surely won him some points over the years – even if Peach did return the favour in *Super Princess Peach* (2005).

21

LUIGI

Oh, brother! Being the sibling of gaming's most famous superstar can be a heavy burden to bear. But Luigi carries it well, even managing to occasionally step out of Mario's shadow and into some all-time-classic games of his own.

Most-liked tweet about Luigi

On 8 Aug 2018, Nintendo killed Luigi... well, kind of. In a *Super Smash Bros. Ultimate* Direct video, Luigi was felled by Death's scythe (the same Death from Konami's *Castlevania* series, no less). It left Luigi in a heap on the floor, while his spirit fretted around his body. To reassure worried fans, Nintendo's @NintendoUKVS account tweeted "Luigi is okay" – a message that had been liked 81,220 times as of 5 Feb 2019.

NEXT APPEARANCE

In the tentatively titled *Luigi's Mansion 3*, our green-clad ghost-hunter will brandish the all-new Poltergust G-00. Created once more by Professor E. Gadd, the G-00 model fires plungers, has a built-in Strobulb (in action above) and even uses jet propulsion to boost Luigi into the air!

LOVE STORY

For humble plumbers, Mario and Luigi certainly aim high in the romantic stakes. Luigi's yearnings for Princess Daisy have long been suspected by gamers, but never-confirmed by Nintendo. Perhaps poor Luigi is destined to remain in the friend zone?

First game to star Luigi as the sole hero

In *Mario is Missing!*, an educational title that was published by Nintendo in 1993, Mario is kidnapped by Bowser. Roll up Luigi (and Yoshi) to save the day!

Fastest co-op completion of *Luigi's Mansion* for Nintendo 3DS

Teaming up on 2018's 3DS re-release, the USA's "Super" and "Switchmaster64" poltergusted their way through the ghostly inhabitants of *Luigi's Mansion* in 1 hr 35 min 35 sec. Their time, as verified by Speedrun, was recorded on 4 Nov 2018.

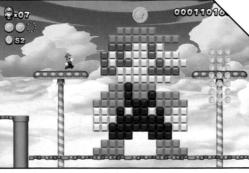

Fastest completion of *New Super Luigi U*

With its short courses designed to be completed in 100 sec or less, *New Super Luigi U* (2013) is ideal for speed-runners. On 14 Jan 2019, in a masterclass of leaping, gliding, sliding and exploiting shortcuts, American "Mchan338" completed the game in 26 min 23 sec. "First attempt of the day and PB'd!" posted the triumphant gamer on Speedrun.

EVOLUTION

Luigi has come a long way since his debut in 1983, but those green overalls make the taller *Mario* brother immediately identifiable, no matter what console he's appearing on.

Super Mario Bros. (1985)

Super Mario Bros. 2 (1988)

Super Mario Bros. 3 (1988)

Super Mario World (1990)

Luigi's Mansion (2001)

Super Mario 64 DS (2004)

New Super Luigi U (2013)

Luigi's Mansion: Dark Moon (2013)

BEST-SELLING LUIGI VIDEOGAME

From time to time, Nintendo sees fit to hand Luigi a lead role – as is the case in the spooktacular *Luigi's Mansion* franchise. The first game in the series sold a very respectable 3.6 million copies. But Luigi's best-selling escapade by far is *Luigi's Mansion: Dark Moon* (2013) on the Nintendo 3DS. As of 4 Feb 2019, it had racked up sales of 5.44 million copies, according to VGChartz. 3DS owners were able to use the handheld's 3D effect to see the game's ghostly denizens in an entirely new dimension.

First *Mario* platformer not to feature Mario

In 2013, to celebrate the 30th anniversary of the videogame debut of Luigi, Nintendo released the *New Super Luigi U* expansion pack for *New Super Mario Bros. Wii U*. Mario wasn't invited to the celebrations, however, with the platform game living up to its name as an all-Luigi affair.

23

MEGA MAN

Capcom created a gaming icon for the ages when *Mega Man* was released back in 1987. But even the company couldn't have predicted the rise of their robotic mascot, or guessed at the number of titles and different genres their blue hero would appear in.

First *Mega Man* film cameo

The Wizard (1989) was no film classic, but it did show respect to games and gamers. Nintendo's *Super Mario Bros. 3* and *Metroid* both featured, but there's also a blink-and-you'll-miss-it appearance from *Mega Man 2*.

First appearance of Rush in a *Mega Man* game

Mega Man's faithful robotic canine companion Rush made his debut in *Mega Man 3* (1990). Like most dogs, he loves chewing on a bone, but unlike most (OK, any) dogs, he's able to help out during adventures by turning into a submarine and a hoverboard. In later games he learns even more tricks. Good boy!

NEMESIS

Years of being in the shadow of fellow roboticist Dr Light led Dr Wily to start reprogramming robots for world domination. Thankfully, none of his creations can ever match Dr Light's Mega Man.

First *Mega Man* costume

Felicia of *Darkstalkers* (1994) fame dressed to impress as Mega Man in Capcom's 1997 fighting game *Super Gem Fighter: Mini Mix*.

Fastest completion of *Mega Man*

Demonstrating how popular 1987's classic still is, "COOLKID" (SWE) set a new "glitchless" fastest time on 28 Jan 2019. He took just 22 min 33 sec, as verified by *Mega Man* RTA Leaderboards.

Fastest completion of *Mega Man 3*

Canadian gamer "ColonelFatso" set the speed-running standard on *Mega Man 3* with a blistering time of 33 min 42 sec on 13 Mar 2019. Previous record holder "fastatcc" said "great job Fatso!".

Fastest completion of *Mega Man 4*

A few players are starting to dip under 38 min in their *Mega Man 4* runs, but it's "Chelney" heading the field. The Canadian gamer's speedy 37 min 17 sec was verified on 8 Mar 2017.

Fastest completion of *Mega Man 7*

The USA's "almondcity" set the fastest time on *Mega Man 7* – our hero's first outing on the Super Nintendo console. The American took 40 min 53 sec on 14 Jul 2018 to foil Dr Wily.

BOSS FIGHT

Over the years, and across 11 main-series games, Dr Wily has come up with all kinds of fiendish robotic designs with which to finally overcome Mega Man. Here's a selection of some of our favourites.

Yellow Devil

Mega Man (1987)

Metal Man

Mega Man 2 (1988)

Shadow Man

Mega Man 3 (1990)

Slash Man

Mega Man 7 (1995)

Sword Man

Mega Man 8 (1996)

Splash Woman

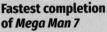
Mega Man 9 (2008)

Block Man

Mega Man 11 (2018)

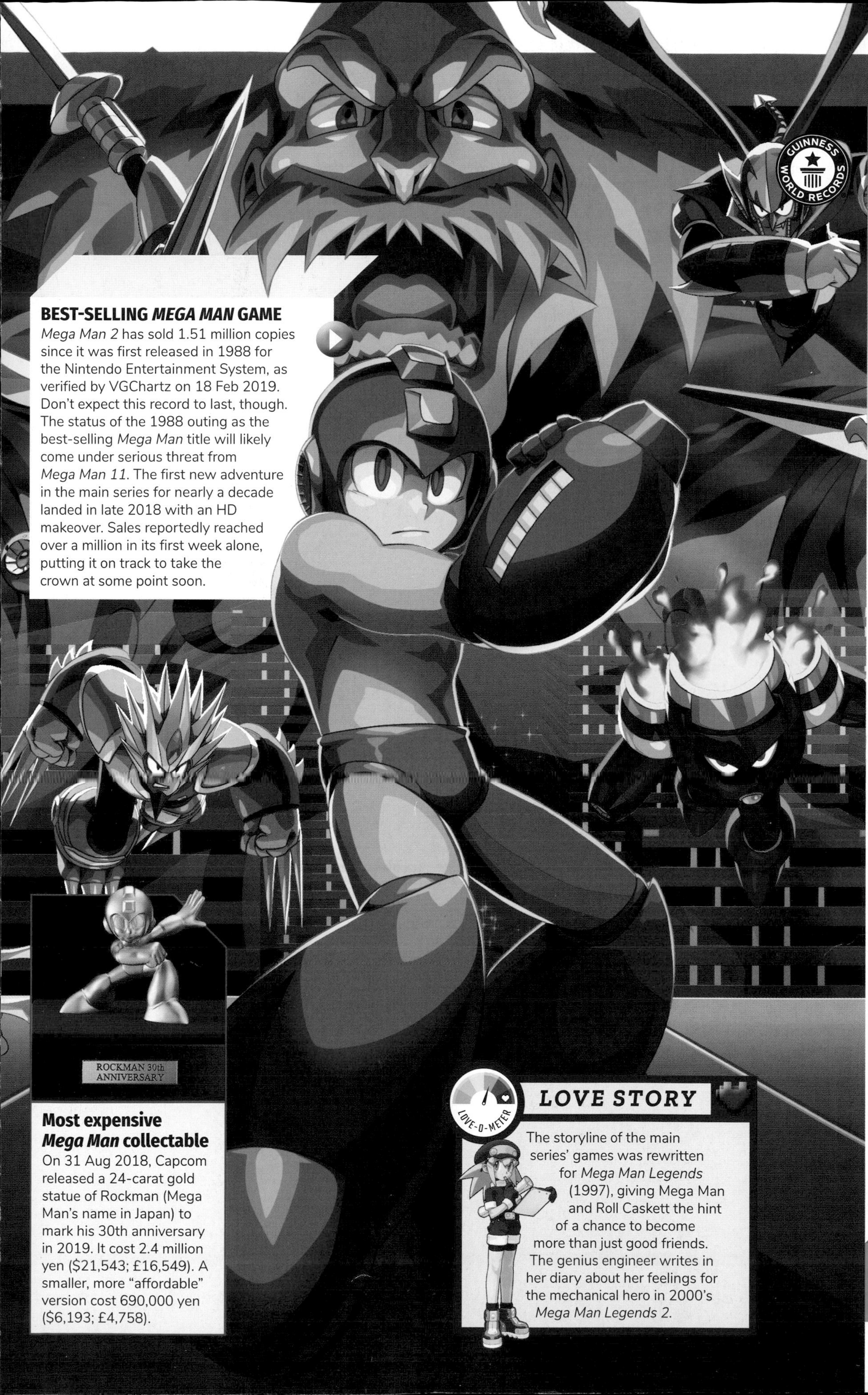

BEST-SELLING *MEGA MAN* GAME

Mega Man 2 has sold 1.51 million copies since it was first released in 1988 for the Nintendo Entertainment System, as verified by VGChartz on 18 Feb 2019. Don't expect this record to last, though. The status of the 1988 outing as the best-selling *Mega Man* title will likely come under serious threat from *Mega Man 11*. The first new adventure in the main series for nearly a decade landed in late 2018 with an HD makeover. Sales reportedly reached over a million in its first week alone, putting it on track to take the crown at some point soon.

ROCKMAN 30th ANNIVERSARY

Most expensive *Mega Man* collectable

On 31 Aug 2018, Capcom released a 24-carat gold statue of Rockman (Mega Man's name in Japan) to mark his 30th anniversary in 2019. It cost 2.4 million yen ($21,543; £16,549). A smaller, more "affordable" version cost 690,000 yen ($6,193; £4,758).

LOVE-O-METER

LOVE STORY

The storyline of the main series' games was rewritten for *Mega Man Legends* (1997), giving Mega Man and Roll Caskett the hint of a chance to become more than just good friends. The genius engineer writes in her diary about her feelings for the mechanical hero in 2000's *Mega Man Legends 2*.

25

SONIC

Sega's spiky blue speedster first raced on to our screens in 1991, wowing players and rivalling the popularity of Super Mario. Relations between hedgehog and plumber have since thawed, but that doesn't mean that Sonic has let up on the pace...

Most appearances for a third-party character in *Super Smash Bros.* (SSB)

Once upon a time, it was unthinkable that Sonic would share a stage with Mario, but these days they regularly appear in *SSB*. Since his debut in *SSB Brawl* (2008), Sega's icon has been a stalwart of the series, with *Ultimate* (2018) being his third appearance – that's more than any other non-Nintendo character.

NEMESIS ☠

Whether you know him as Dr Robotnik or Eggman depends on when and where you first played *Sonic*. Whatever you call him, the mad scientist and his dastardly machines are an ever-present threat to Sonic and his friends.

First pinball spin-off of a console game

Following the popularity of Casino Night Zone in *Sonic 2* (1992), in which the hedgehog became a living pinball, Sega created *Sonic Spinball*. Released on 18 Nov 1993, it pipped the similar *Kirby's Pinball Land* (Nintendo) by 12 days.

SUPPORTING CAST

Over the years, our quicksilver hero has picked up a whole host of allies (and the odd enemy) on his high-octane travels. Here, we celebrate the characters that are only too happy to come along on Sonic's roller-coaster ride.

Miles "Tails" Prower has been with Sonic since the early days.

Tails

Knuckles

The red echidna is also the guardian of the Master Emerald.

GREEN THRILLS...

The classic Green Hill Zone is the **most recurring level in a** *Sonic* **videogame series**, appearing in 18 titles since Sonic's debut in 1991.

The **fastest completion of Green Hill Zone 1 in** *Sonic Mania Plus* **(as Sonic)** was achieved by "Joeybaby69" (USA) in 27.87 sec on 24 Jul 2018, as verified by Speedrun.

First videogame in a popcorn machine

Sonic has appeared on many platforms, but his foray on to a popcorn machine must count among the strangest. On 13 Apr 1993, Sega issued the *Segasonic Popcorn Shop*, a vending machine with a game in which Sonic makes popcorn to thwart Eggman. It provided three flavours: salt, butter and curry.

Sonic the Hedgehog ✓
@sonic_hedgehog

The OFFICIAL Twitter feed for news about all things Sonic. We also like memes.

MOST FOLLOWED VIDEOGAME CHARACTER ON TWITTER

As of 12 Feb 2019, the official Twitter account for Sonic the Hedgehog (@sonic_hedgehog) had 5,774,195 followers. The tweets are written as if they're from the mouth of Sonic himself. The account's popularity was helped by the 2017 release of *Sonic Mania*, the **most critically acclaimed *Sonic the Hedgehog* title**. Also as of 12 Feb 2019, the game had an average score of 87.02% across 40 reviews on GameRankings, with critics happy to see the spiky mascot returning to his 2D roots.

Shadow the Hedgehog

Imagine Sonic with firearms and a bad temper and you have Shadow.

Silver the Hedgehog

Protecting the future is all that matters to this time-traveller.

Rouge the Bat

This jewel thief is happy to help Sonic out – when it suits her.

290 ISSUES

Published by Archie Comics, *Sonic the Hedgehog* was the **longest-running comic series based on a videogame character**. It first appeared in Jul 1993 and its 290th (and last) edition was printed on 28 Dec 2016. A spin-off, *Sonic Universe*, was published by Archie Comics from Feb 2009 to Jan 2017.

LOVE STORY

LOVE-O-METER

Friendship and admiration have yet to turn into romance between Sonic and Sally Acorn (right), who is busy as a freedom-fighting chipmunk. This pleases Amy Rose (left), who is convinced (mostly in her own mind) that she is destined to be with Sonic – and woe betide anyone who tries to get in her way!

27

CRASH BANDICOOT

Though no longer PlayStation's mascot, Crash cemented his megastar status in the mid-1990s as the poster boy of the PSOne. Since then, he's spun himself on to all kinds of consoles and across a wide variety of gaming genres.

NEMESIS

He might be grinning, but Dr Neo Cortex really isn't winning. The mad scientist's Evolvo-Ray was supposed to create a leader for his evil army. But instead it created Crash, who has been a thorn in Cortex's side ever since!

First non-Japanese PlayStation title to sell over one million in Japan

Crash Bandicoot 3: Warped (Sony, 1998) was the first western-developed PSOne title to break the seven-figure sales mark in Japan. Naughty Dog, the studio that developed *Crash*, was awarded Japan's "Platinum Prize" in Jun 1999, something Naughty Dog celebrates on its website even now.

Fastest "full trilogy" any% completion of *N. Sane Trilogy*

Demonstrating complete mastery of Crash's moves, Uruguay's "cameronvengenz" dashed through the entire *Crash Bandicoot: N. Sane Trilogy* (Activision, 2017) on PC in 2 hr 9 min 59 sec. His cumulative time through the HD remasters of *Crash Bandicoot* 1, 2 and 3 was verified by Speedrun on 13 Jan 2019.

SNAPSHOT

Crash had a surprise game-in-game cameo in *Uncharted 4: A Thief's End* (Sony, 2016). What better way for *Uncharted*'s Nate and Elena to unwind after a hard day's adventuring than with a game of Crash's first PSOne outing?

Largest bandicoot

At about 1.4 m (4 ft 7 in) tall and weighing an estimated 45 kg (99 lb), Crash is quite a bit larger than the biggest real-world bandicoot. That honour falls to the giant bandicoot (*Peroryctes broadbenti*), a species that lives in the forests of Papua New Guinea and weighs up to 5 kg (11 lb).

EVOLUTION

Crash's early titles raised the bar for 3D graphics on the PSOne. Since then, he's gone from standard to high definition, tried kart racing and has even been cast in plastic as a *Skylanders* figure.

Crash Bandicoot (1996)

Cortex Strikes Back (1997)

Warped (1998)

Crash Team Racing (1999)

The Wrath of Cortex (2001)

Crash of the Titans (2007)

Skylanders: Imaginators (2016)

N. Sane Trilogy (2017)

Fastest any% warpless completion of *Crash Team Racing*

Serbian gamer "BlitzPhoenix98" put the pedal to the metal on 21 Dec 2018. He completed an any% warpless run of the bandicoot's 1999 racer in just 50 min 35 sec, as verified by Speedrun.

MOST SUCCESSFUL TRILOGY STARRING A PLAYSTATION-EXCLUSIVE CHARACTER

Forget the likes of Nathan Drake, Kratos and Spyro because, as of 5 Feb 2019, the PlayStation-exclusive character with the most successful trilogy of games is Crash. As verified by VGChartz, his original Sony-published trilogy (comprising *Crash Bandicoot*, *Cortex Strikes Back* and *Warped*) sold 21.53 million copies. It's no wonder that Activision (the current publisher of *Crash* games) saw fit to capitalize on the trilogy's success by releasing the *N. Sane Trilogy* HD remaster in 2017.

PIKACHU

It was as long ago as the mid-1990s that Pikachu struck the gaming world like a thunderbolt. These days, he's not only the star of *Pokémon* games, he's also the face of TV shows, toys, books and even major Hollywood movies.

NEXT APPEARANCE

Pokémon Sword and its partner title *Shield* are the next major releases in the world of *Pokémon*. Set to be out in late 2019 for the Switch, they'll transport players to the forested and mountainous land of Galar.

Cover star

Pikachu's image has appeared on 30 unique game devices – the **most physical appearances on official consoles**. His first was on 1998's Pokémon Center Tokyo Edition Game Boy Light (above top left). His latest was on the *Super Smash Bros. Ultimate*-themed Switch on 7 Dec 2018 (above bottom left).

3 HR 24 MIN 27 SEC

Denmark's "Retrotato" and "Chibidesuu" proved that catching Pokémon is better done in pairs as they set the **fastest co-op completion of *Pokémon Let's Go, Pikachu!/Eevee!*** Strong teamwork and synchronization helped them dip under 3 hr 25 min, as verified by Speedrun on 11 Jan 2019.

EVOLUTION

Pikachu has such a long history in the gaming universe that his debut was in the black-and-white world of the Game Boy. Things have moved on since then, with Pikachu first going full colour, before eventually going full HD.

Pokémon
Red and *Blue*

Game Boy
(1996)

Pokémon
Gold and *Silver*

Game Boy Color
(1999)

Pokémon
Ruby and *Sapphire*

Game Boy Advance
(2002)

Highest national spend on *Pokémon GO*

Between its initial release in Jul 2016 and 25 Sep 2018, *Pokémon GO* had generated a cool $2 bn (£1.53 bn) in revenue from in-game purchases. According to data-tracking site Apptopia, over a third (33.5%) of that came from Japan – the ancestral home of *Pokémon*. American gamers spent the next most at 27.5%.

Largest human image of a *Pokémon*

On 26 Nov 2017, in Yoshinogari Historical Park, Saga, Japan, 994 people assembled in colour-coded clothing to create one big Pikachu. It should have been 1,000 (to match the number of episodes of the TV show at the time), but six people were disqualified for sitting down!

MOST UBIQUITOUS VIDEOGAME RPG CHARACTER

Since debuting in 1996's *Pokémon Red* and *Blue*, Pikachu has been an electrifying presence. As of 7 Dec 2018 and the release of *Super Smash Bros. Ultimate*, Pikachu has appeared in 71 games. That covers the less-well-known titles, such as *Hey You, Pikachu!* (1998) and *PokéPark Wii: Pikachu's Adventure* (2009), up to his starring role in *Pokémon: Let's Go, Pikachu!* (2018) for the Switch. His tally is bound to increase, with *Pokémon Sword* and *Shield* (see left) set to be released in 2019.

Pokémon *Diamond* and *Pearl*	*Pokémon* *Black* and *White*	*Pokémon* *X* and *Y*	*Let's Go, Pikachu!* and *Let's Go, Eevee!*
Nintendo DS (2006)	Nintendo DS (2010)	Nintendo 3DS (2013)	Nintendo Switch (2018)

First live-action *Pokémon* film

Released in the US on 10 May 2019, *Pokémon: Detective Pikachu* was the first *Pokémon* movie to be live-action rather than a cartoon. Its Pokémon were reimagined so they could convincingly share the big screen with humans in real-world sets. Ryan Reynolds lent his voice to Pikachu.

LOVE STORY

A big deal was made when the "A Plethora of Pikachu!" episode of the *Pokémon* TV show was aired in Japan on 7 Oct 2018. Rumour had it that Ash's Pikachu would finally find love. In the end, though, sparks between Pikachu and Kurin (left) flew for just an instant, leaving Pikachu's fans disappointed.

GORDON FREEMAN

The physicist-turned-hero hasn't set foot in a new game since 2007, but the legacy of *Half-Life* is such that we didn't hesitate when placing Gordon Freeman into this chapter. Just don't ask the famously silent character when *Half-Life 3* is coming out...

First game released by Valve Corporation

Founded by ex-Microsoft employees Gabe Newell and Mike Harrington in 1996, Valve (which also owns the online gaming service Steam) is now one of the industry's most influential companies. Much of that success flowed from *Half-Life*, which changed first-person shooters for ever after its launch on 19 Nov 1998.

NEMESIS ☠

G-Man inspires as many questions as answers. Whose side is he on? Is he a mysterious ally or is he Gordon Freeman's puppet master? And is the dimension-hopping shadowy figure even human? Your guess is as good as ours.

Longest protest over a game delay

Two unidentified Canadian *Half-Life* fans picketed Valve's Seattle offices for two days in 2011, desperate to gain information on when *Half-Life 3* might be released. Although Valve boss Gabe Newell (above right) met the fans and gave them snacks, he didn't reveal any further details about this much-anticipated game (and still hasn't).

WEAPON SELECT

Gordon Freeman's most famous weapon might be his trusty crowbar, but bring a crowbar to a gunfight and even he might occasionally struggle. Here, we detail the deadly weaponry from the original *Half-Life*, both from our planet and beyond...

Crowbar
The legend, the leverage.

Pistol
Lacking in power, but handy at a pinch.

.357 Magnum
Deadly, but ammo is always at a premium.

First videogame with full closed captioning

Even though Gordon Freeman is famously silent, *Half-Life 2* (2004) offered full closed captioning. As well as character speech (right), dynamic in-game actions also prompt subtitles. For example, "[Boom!]" flashes up on screen every time a grenade explodes.

Welcome. Welcome to City 17.

Rarest achievement in *Half-Life 2*

According to Steam, *Half-Life 2*'s "Lambda Locator" achievement had been unlocked by just 2.6% of PC players as of 6 Feb 2019. The achievement is granted to those who discover all 45 caches of bonus equipment hidden throughout the game's environments. Each is marked by a solitary Lambda character (right).

14 YEARS 31 DAYS...

The *Black Mesa* fan remake of *Half-Life* was first announced on 1 Mar 2005. On 14 Sep 2012, a version was issued as a free download. It contained all the chapters of the original game, with the exception of the final "Xen" stage. On 19 Nov 2018, the Crowbar Collective said the missing chapter would finally be released in Q2 of 2019. Assuming the game is put out on 1 Apr 2019 (the earliest Q2 2019 date), the development period will have been 14 years 31 days. Whatever the final waiting time, *Black Mesa* will have had the **longest development period for a fan-made videogame**.

Shotgun	Black Mesa Crossbow	Tau Cannon	Hivehand	Snark
For when aliens get up close and personal.	Damage at a distance for the quiet assassin.	Walls are no barrier to this particle-beam.	Its "hornets" chase foes around corners.	No gun? Throw this hungry alien instead!

SNAPSHOT

The scripted introduction to 1998's *Half-Life* paved the way for narrative-led first-person shooters. Gordon Freeman's monorail trip through the Black Mesa Research Facility was grand in scope and scale, but it also gave players a tantalizing glimpse of the areas they'd be able to explore later in the game.

11,107,520 VIEWS

As of 6 Feb 2019, "HALF LIFE IN 60 SECONDS" by German YouTuber "rompkows" had been viewed over 11 million times, making it the **most popular Gordon Freeman fan film**. The animation has no footage from the actual games, but instead uses *South Park*-style animation to re-tell the plots of both *Half-Life* and *Half-Life 2*.

MAPPIN' ASSASSINS

From the minarets of the Holy Land to the pirate coves of the Caribbean, the *Assassin's Creed* series has taken us to many glamorous places and time periods. So hop into the Animus for some killer records on our grand tour of assassination destinations.

Assassin's Creed Syndicate
DATE SET: 1868–88
LOCATION: London, UK

Climbing Big Ben is fun in *Syndicate*, but assassins can't neglect the job in hand. As of 25 Feb 2019, Xbox One gamer "GENERALESUPREMO" had taken ruthlessness to a new level with a total kill count of 39,659 – the **most kills by any *Assassin's Creed Syndicate* player**, according to TrueAchievements.

Assassin's Creed Unity
DATE SET: 1789–93
LOCATION: France

Unity introduced time shifts that dropped the lead character, Arno Victor Dorian, into different time periods. One example sees Dorian fast-forwarded into 1944 – straight into the midst of World War II – where he can climb the Eiffel Tower.

Assassin's Creed III
DATE SET: 1760–83
LOCATION: Boston, USA

Players who explore Boston in *Assassin's Creed III* will come across the Old North Church (pictured). They might also bump into Shaun Hastings, a character voiced by the UK's Danny Wallace. He has the **most voiceover performances in the series**, having lent his voice to seven entries.

Assassin's Creed IV: Black Flag
DATE SET: 1715–22
LOCATION: The Caribbean

Black Flag is the **first Assassin's Creed game with unlockable sea shanties**. Players can collect them in 34 locations around the game's world. One of the shanties is to be found in the shadow of the Basilica Menor de San Francisco de Asis in modern-day Havana, Cuba.

Assassin's Creed II
DATE SET: 1476–99
LOCATION: Italy

Players with nerves of steel can take the **highest leap of faith in** *Assassin's Creed II*. It is from the Campanile di Giotto, the bell tower of the Basilica di Santa Maria del Fiore in Florence (far left), which is 84.7 m (277 ft 10 in) tall. Leaping unlocks the "High Dive" achievement.

Assassin's Creed Odyssey
DATE SET: 431 BCE
LOCATION: Greece

Odyssey's recreation of ancient Greece covers a lot of ground and includes plenty of famous buildings, such as the Parthenon. In fact, it's the **largest explorable land mass in an** *Assassin's Creed* **title**. YouTuber Dimitris Galatas used clever software and in-game measurements to determine that it covered a colossal 256.38 km² (98.98 sq mi)!

Assassin's Creed Origins
DATE SET: 49–47 BCE
LOCATION: Cairo, Egypt

When they're not exploring the wonders of the Great Pyramid, *Origins* players can avenge the deaths of other gamers by hunting down their killer. As of 25 Feb 2019, "EagererJam679" was the **most vengeful**, having got payback on 989 occasions.

Assassin's Creed
DATE SET: 1191
LOCATION: The Holy Land

In the series' first outing, Altaïr can explore the Dome of the Rock (Qubbat al-Sakhra). The famous Islamic shrine provides the backdrop to one of the franchise's most dramatic leaps of faith, as Altaïr dives from its summit.

Largest *Assassin's Creed* memorabilia collection

Italy's Carlo Prisco began collecting *Assassin's Creed* items in 2007. Over the past dozen years, the native of Pozzuoli in Naples – the famous port and city that features in *Assassin's Creed: Brotherhood* (2010) – has amassed a hoard that runs to 1,030 items, as verified on 10 Feb 2019. Among the pieces are a shield, helmet and spear straight from *Assassin's Creed Odyssey* (pictured).

ROLE-PLAYERS

The brave heroes in this chapter chase every horizon, take on the most ferocious monsters and, of course, will sacrifice themselves without a moment's hesitation if it means stopping evil in its tracks.

An epic journey ends
On 9 Mar 2019, "Katia Sae" (aka Ethan Richards, USA) became the **first player to explore all reachable systems in *EVE Online* without a single combat loss**. It was the end of an intergalactic journey for the explorer that started on 1 Dec 2009 and lasted for 9 years 98 days. In that time, he visited all 7,508 New Eden solar systems (not including the 230 unreachable Jove systems) in CCP Games' 2003 title. "The sandbox nature of the immersive universe of New Eden allowed me to create my own story," said Ethan.

COMING UP ▶▶▶

SORA

As the spark of light against the evil threat posed by the Heartless, there's plenty of weight on Sora's young shoulders in the *Kingdom Hearts* series. But with Goofy, Donald Duck and an entourage of famous Disney characters by his side, he's able to stand tall.

SNAPSHOT

One of the fabulous quirks of the *Kingdom Hearts* series is that Sora, Donald and Goofy take on the physical attributes of whatever Disney world they're visiting. This was taken to a particularly cute conclusion during *Kingdom Hearts II*, when Sora was transformed into a lion cub – not unlike *The Lion King*'s Simba.

Most hearts carried by a *Kingdom Hearts* character
Much of Sora's power comes from his ability to absorb the "hearts" of the game's characters (see above). Sora has safeguarded, or been a conduit for, as many as six hearts other than his own: Ventus, Vanitas, Kairi, Xion, Roxas and Riku. This gives Sora the unique ability to wield several Keyblades to help thwart the Heartless.

Fastest-selling *Kingdom Hearts* videogame
Proving that Disney magic is more popular than ever, Square Enix took to Twitter to confirm that *Kingdom Hearts III* had shipped over 5 million units – covering physical and digital sales – after just one week on sale, following its worldwide release on 29 Jan 2019. This means that the JRPG is a near certainty to pass the 6.4 million lifetime sales of *Kingdom Hearts* (2002), the series' best-selling title so far.

Best-selling character crossover RPG series
Disney Infinity and *LEGO® Dimensions* are blockbuster crossovers, but both still have to look up to the *Kingdom Hearts* series. As of 18 Feb 2019, it had sold 27.27 million units, according to VGChartz. With *Kingdom Hearts III* still selling well (see above left), the gap's set to grow even wider.

NEMESIS

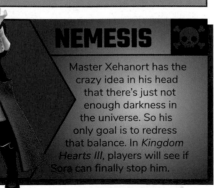

Master Xehanort has the crazy idea in his head that there's just not enough darkness in the universe. So his only goal is to redress that balance. In *Kingdom Hearts III*, players will see if Sora can finally stop him.

BOSS FIGHT
The *Kingdom Hearts* franchise has raided Disney's animated archives for iconic enemies. No matter what film they're from, all are united by being among the big screen's most despised villains.

Hades

from *Hercules*

Hans

from *Frozen*

Mother Gothel

from *Tangled*

Maleficent

from *Sleeping Beauty*

Randy

from *Monsters, Inc.*

Zurg

from *Toy Story*

MOST APPEARANCES AS THE HERO IN SQUARE ENIX RPGS

Sora is the king of Square Enix role-playing games. Across the many RPGs to emerge from the Enix Corporation and Square, which combined in 2003 to become Square Enix, the upbeat teenager has taken centre stage more times than anyone else. He has the lead role in six *Kingdom Hearts* adventures: *Kingdom Hearts* (2002), *Chain of Memories* (2004), *Kingdom Hearts II* (2005), *Birth by Sleep* (2010), *Kingdom Hearts 3D: Dream Drop Distance* (2012) and *Kingdom Hearts III* (2019).

2 HR 57 MIN 19 SEC

On 19 May 2017, "Bizkit047" (USA) achieved the **fastest "Level 1 Proud" run** of *Kingdom Hearts HD 1.5 ReMIX*, going under three hours. It was especially notable given how tough "Proud" difficulty is. The attempt raised funds for a mental-health charity.

Most critically acclaimed *Kingdom Hearts* game

Despite a challenge from *Kingdom Hearts III*, 2005's *Kingdom Hearts II* has held on as the series' top-scoring title. As verified by GameRankings on 18 Feb 2019, it scored an average of 87.46%. *Kingdom Hearts III* averaged 83.28%.

CLOUD STRIFE

The spiky-haired lead of *Final Fantasy VII* (1997) was the JRPG hero who bridged the gap between east and west. Never before had a Japanese role-playing game been released to such worldwide acclaim and popularity.

$145 MILLION

In order to produce Cloud's spectacular journey in *Final Fantasy VII*, its then-publisher Square allocated a combined development and marketing budget of $145 m (£90.5 m) – making it the **costliest JRPG** ever. It was a gamble, but, as history shows, the investment paid off.

First JRPG hero in a fighting game

A chocobo appeared in Square's 1997 fighting game *Tobal 2,* but it was Cloud who became the first JRPG hero to enter a fighting arena. He made his fighting-game debut in Namco's *Ehrgeiz* (1998) and was joined by *FFVII* heroine Tifa Lockhart.

Largest replica videogame sword

In May 2013, Hollywood armourer Tony Swatton created a metal replica of Cloud Strife's *FFVII* Buster Sword. It is 2.59 m (8 ft 5 in) long and made from aluminium, bronze and steel. The whole thing weighs a hefty 21.65 kg (47 lb 11 oz)!

SUPPORTING CAST

Even Cloud can't shoulder the weight of saving the world by himself. Along the way, eco-warriors, magical beasts and even a remote-controlled toy cat will rally to his side to stop Sephiroth. The journey won't be without its share of heartbreak, though...

Tifa Lockhart   **Barret Wallace**   **Aerith Gainsborough**

NEMESIS ☠

Sephiroth's attempts to piece together his past trigger the apocalyptic events of *FFVII* and instigate some of gaming's most memorable moments. For a villain with only a few scenes, he left a huge, lasting impression.

First JRPG hero to have a scent named after them

At the 2009 Tokyo Game Show, Square Enix unveiled an unusual new addition to its official range of products: the Cloud Strife Eau de Toilette. Priced at 7,140 yen ($78.38; £47.80) per 50 ml bottle, the perfume carried a scent described as "refreshing, floral, fruity and oriental". Sephiroth (*FFVII*), Lightning (*FFXIII*) and Noctis (*FFXV*) also have their own special scents.

MOST IN-GAME APPEARANCES BY A *FINAL FANTASY* HERO

As fans of *FF* know, certain characters such as Cid, Cactuar and Gilgamesh recur throughout the series. However, Cloud's appearances in 28 games go far beyond *FF*. He did return for more *Final Fantasy* in *Dirge of Cerberus* (2006) and *Crisis Core* (2007), but he also spread his wings. He appeared in *Kingdom Hearts* (Square Enix, 2002) and took up arms in Nintendo's *Super Smash Bros. for Wii U* (2014) and *Ultimate* (2018).

| Red XIII | Cait Sith | Cid Highwind | Yuffie Kisaragi | Vincent Valentine |

NEXT APPEARANCE

The *Final Fantasy VII Remake* exists – it was announced by Square Enix during Sony's now-legendary press conference at E3 2015 – but the wait goes on for its release. All we know for certain is that it will reconstruct the events of *FFVII*, but this time with fabulous visuals. Whenever it drops, expect Cloud to star.

11 MILLION SALES

Since its PSOne debut in 1997, the original *FFVII* has been adapted for all kinds of platforms, including PS4, PC, iOS and Android – with Xbox One and Switch versions to follow. As of 19 Feb 2019, it's the **best-selling JRPG on home consoles**, with 11 million copies sold according to Square Enix (and surely more once those Switch and Xbox One sales are confirmed).

GERALT OF RIVIA

Adapting *The Witcher* from its fantasy-novel source material into one of the world's best-loved RPGs has led to plaudits and sales aplenty for CD Projekt Red. And at the centre of that success? Who else but the heroic, and ever-cynical, Geralt of Rivia.

First *Witcher* character to feature in another publisher's game

Geralt likes to moan about his dislike of portals, but he still transported to another gaming universe for Bandai Namco's *SoulCalibur VI* on 19 Oct 2018. Unhappily (for him), he also crossed over to Capcom's *Monster Hunter World* on 8 Feb 2019.

92.23%

Geralt's sprawling journey in *The Witcher III: Wild Hunt* (2015) remains the **most critically acclaimed action RPG for eighth-gen consoles**. As of 18 Feb 2019, the PS4 version scored 92.23% (from 51 reviews) on GameRankings. One reviewer called it a "pure delight for any RPG and fantasy fan".

Rarest achievement in *The Witcher III: Wild Hunt*

"Master Marksman" requires players to kill 50 enemies – human, monster or other – by striking them in the head with a crossbow bolt. As of 18 Feb 2019, only 6,320 (7%) of 96,311 tracked gamers had unlocked it, according to TrueAchievements.

Radovid's Deck
NORTHERN REALMS / 30 cards / Ready to play

ALL   SPECIAL   TROOP   CHARACTER   HERO

Clear board   TOGGLE FILTER   Zoom Card

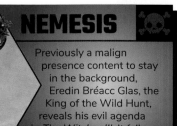

NEMESIS

Previously a malign presence content to stay in the background, Eredin Bréacc Glas, the King of the Wild Hunt, reveals his evil agenda in *The Witcher III*. It falls to Geralt and Ciri to unite against his tyranny.

$112,736.82

Geralt is the biggest badass in the *Witcher* games but when it comes to playing the digital card game *Gwent*, current top dog is the UK's "Freddybabes" (aka Fred Bird). As of 18 Feb 2019, the **highest-earning *Gwent* esports player** had won $112,736 (£87,408) in prize money from nine tournaments, according to Esportsearnings.

POWER-UP

Geralt can cast one-handed spells called Signs, which are represented by runic symbols. As you progress in *The Witcher III* and Geralt's mastery increases, he's able to learn ever-more destructive Signs to unleash.

Aard

Softens up your foe so that attacks deal more damage.

Igni

Make an opponent hot under the collar with this fiery spell.

Yrden

Slows down your prey to line up the perfect strike.

Quen

Absorb your enemy's best shot with this protective shield.

Axii

Messes with your foe's mind to take them out of the fight.

STRONGEST GWENT CARD IN *THE WITCHER 3: WILD HUNT*

Anyone holding the "Geralt of Rivia" card in *Gwent*, the collectable card game-within-a-game playable in *The Witcher III: Wild Hunt*, is in an enviable position. To get it, players have to defeat Thaler in the "Old Pals" quest. Once played in a game of *Gwent*, it's able to fight off the effects of other cards and possesses the highest possible strength of 15. The top trump is matched only by the card of his protégée, Cirilla Fiona Elen Riannon (whom fans will know better as Ciri).

LOVE STORY

LOVE-O-METER

Geralt's heart is torn between two women, Triss (left) and Yennefer (right). As the player, it's up to you to decide who, if either, he'll finally fall for. But a word of warning: make a choice and keep to it, or heartache could await our hero.

Most viewed original *The Witcher* fan film

Directed by Leo Kei Angelos (USA), "THE WITCHER | Fan Film" had notched up 1,565,618 views on YouTube as of 18 Feb 2019. It stars Germany's "Maul Cosplay" (aka Ben Schamma, right), who is also an official Geralt cosplayer. In the four-minute short, Geralt and Triss take on the evil Cursed Knight.

43

COMMANDER SHEPARD

Whether you've chosen to play as "Maleshep" or "Femshep", the daunting task that confronts Commander Shepard in EA's *Mass Effect* series stays the same – saving all life across the galaxy from total annihilation.

NEMESIS

The secretive Illusive Man will do anything to make humanity the dominant force among the galaxy's races. When it suits his agenda, he's even known to aid Shepard, but this master manipulator should never be trusted.

A moral victory

Demonstrating the heroic side of its players, Paragon is the **most popular morality trait in *Mass Effect 3***. In Mar 2013, EA released an infographic revealing a 64.5% to 35.5% split between the merciful Paragon and the ruthless Renegade traits.

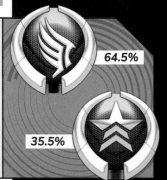

64.5%

35.5%

Fastest completion of *Mass Effect 3*

On 19 Apr 2017, Belgian speedster "LeXtruX" blasted through a New Game+ "Narrative" (easy difficulty) run in a blistering time of 2 hr 52 min 29 sec. Commenting on Speedrun, the gamer said that he could go even faster.

SUPPORTING CAST

The crew members of Shepard's ship are an interesting bunch. Among them are genetically modified humans (Miranda), "normal" humans (Kaidan), Turians (Garrus), Asari (Liara), Krogans (Urdnot Wrex) and Quarians (Tali). Each has a unique storyline and some might fall along the way. Much like that of the galaxy, their fate is in your hands.

Miranda

Garrus

LOVE STORY

Depending on who you recruit to your team and who you spend your time with, romance in *Mass Effect* can follow many paths. Don't think your choices are limited just to the same species, either. Shepard is just as likely to find romance with one of his (or her) alien crewmates as one of the humans on board.

First male model cast in a videogame

As you can see, the face of "Maleshep" in the *Mass Effect* series was based on that of male model Mark Vanderloo (NLD). His face might not belong to *your* Shepard, though, because players are invited to alter the face, build and gender of the game's hero before starting.

GUINNESS WORLD RECORDS

MOST CRITICALLY ACCLAIMED ROLE-PLAYING GAME

What is it about the middle entry of a trilogy? *Mass Effect 2* (2010) joined the likes of *The Empire Strikes Back* and *The Godfather Part II* by becoming the darling of the series. As of 20 Feb 2019, BioWare's RPG on Xbox 360 enjoyed an aggregate GameRankings score of 95.77% from 75 reviews. Critics and fans both applauded its revamped combat – which made for a more action-heavy experience compared with its predecessor – as well as its memorable storyline.

Liara	Tali	Kaidan	Urdnot Wrex

First Western RPG content to appear in a JRPG

Major crossover promotions are common now, but one of the earliest was a Square Enix and EA collaboration on 27 Mar 2012. It brought Commander Shepard's iconic N7 armour to *Final Fantasy XIII-2*. *Mass Effect*-inspired outfits could be downloaded for Serah Farron and Noel Kreiss (right).

First astronaut to narrate a videogame

The emotional ending of *Mass Effect 3* is narrated by an alien called the Stargazer. Depending on your choices during the game's finale, the Stargazer's voice will either be that of the second man on the Moon, Buzz Aldrin, or US actress Christine Dunford.

LAST DRAGONBORN

Bethesda's sprawling 2011 RPG *The Elder Scrolls V: Skyrim* introduced us to the Last Dragonborn. You have the freedom to customize your hero's appearance, but it's always his (or her) soul of a dragon that fuels their incredible strength.

NEMESIS ☠

Miraak, the first of all known Dragonborn, is the yin to the Last Dragonborn's yang. His rise to power was fuelled by devouring the souls of dragons, but his arrogance and overconfidence will be his undoing in the end.

Most popular *Skyrim* fan art

They say "a picture is worth a thousand words", but these days it can be worth 25,000 Reddit upvotes, too. That's how popular Simon Forsman's Etch-A-Sketch artwork "A Nord's last thoughts should be of home" has proven (as of 9 Jan 2019) since he first posted it on 11 Feb 2018.

83 YEARS

As a huge fan of Bethesda's RPG, Shirley Curry – aged 83 years as of 2 Apr 2019 – uploaded hundreds of videos of her playing the game to her YouTube channel, making her the **oldest gaming YouTuber**. Bethesda even announced it will immortalize her as an NPC in *The Elder Scrolls VI*.

POWER-UP

Dragon Shouts – magical powers that only the Last Dragonborn and a select few others can unleash – are the ancient commands used to channel the essence of the dragons you defeat while adventuring through *Skyrim*. Here is just a selection of these powerful weapons (and a translation of the words spoken).

Animal Allegiance

RAAN   MIR   TAH

Become Ethereal

FEIM   ZII   GRON

SNAPSHOT 📷

In a baptism of fire for *Skyrim* newbies, the first dragon they must face on their journey is the monstrous Mirmulnir. Fear not, though, as slaying the flame-breathing beast is the key to unlocking the Last Dragonborn's destiny. Upon defeating Mirmulnir, the hero's ability to absorb the power of any dragon is revealed.

Most popular *Skyrim* cosplayer

April Gloria's near-perfect depictions of Aela the Huntress (pictured), Astrid and Mjoll the Lioness have earned her plenty of fans on social media. As of 18 Feb 2019, she had 314,221 followers across Instagram (109,537), Facebook (199,471) and Twitter (5,213).

MOST PLATFORMS FOR AN ACTION RPG VIDEOGAME

Players have their pick of platforms when joining the Last Dragonborn on his quest. *Skyrim* is available on six platforms: PS3, PS4, Xbox 360, Xbox One, Switch and PC. *Skyrim VR* (2018) is also out on the PS VR and PC, as is an audio-only adaptation for the Amazon Alexa smart speaker. "Millions of people every month are playing [*Skyrim*]," said the game's director, Todd Howard. "That's why we keep releasing it."

Fire Breath	Frost Breath	Slow Time	Unrelenting Force
YOL TOOR SHUL	FO KRAH DIIN	TIID KLO UL	FUS RO DAH

First Nintendo crossover in an *Elder Scrolls* game

Skyrim's arrival on the Switch on 17 Nov 2017 brought with it a unique new wardrobe for the Last Dragonborn. Switch owners were able to kit him out with three exclusive items taken straight from the *Legend of Zelda* series, with Link's Master Sword, his blue Champion's Tunic and a Hylian Shield all available.

Most powerful dragon type in *Skyrim*

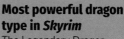

The Legendary Dragon is the fiercest of its kin. Swooping in with the "Dawnguard" DLC, these Level-75 nightmares have insect-like eyes, curved horns and can deal devastating fire and frost attacks. To take one down you'll have to inflict 4,163 points of damage! The good news is that if you live to defeat one, they'll drop epic loot.

47

Late Edition

Liberty City **Today:** hot hot hot – high 73. **Tonight:** cool with a chance of crime. **Tomorrow:** who can tell? Weather map on next page.

Liberty City Times

"All the news that really shouldn't be in print"

A FISTFUL OF DOLLARS

ISSUE 01

LIBERTY CITY TUESDAY 17 SEPTEMBER

FEATURE

Fastest multi-game *GTA* speed-run

GERMANY, 22 Jun 2018. Speed-running sensation "RoK_24" tore through the entire *Grand Theft Auto 3D* trilogy – that's to say *GTA III, GTA: Vice City* and *GTA: San Andreas* – in 6 hr 34 min 4 sec. He played through the PC versions of all three titles, beginning with each game's first story mission and not stopping until the credits rolled.

GTA V LEAVES *CoD* IN ITS DUST

GTA V is officially the **best-selling videogame of the eighth generation**

With his AK-47 pointing this way, Trevor Philips (left) has us at a bit of a disadvantage, so we'd better be careful what we say. But we hope he'll be pleased to find out that, as of 14 Feb 2019, across PS4, Xbox One and PC, sales of *Grand Theft Auto V* put Rockstar's most recent entry well ahead of the competition. Its 29.44 million physical copies sold has burned off both Activision's 2015 title *Call of Duty: Black Ops III* (22.76 million) and EA's 2017 *FIFA 18* (15.02 million).

If that sounds impressive (we really hope it does, Mr Philips),

then bear in mind that the figure doesn't take into account seventh-generation sales. Add in the number of boxed copies sold on the PS3 and the Xbox 360, and the total *GTA V* sales figure rises to 65.62 million. Rockstar's publicly released financial reports, which include digital sales as well as retail sales, suggest that the total figure across all media is nearing 100 million, but the inclusion of digital sales means we can't verify the count using our usual source at VGChartz – no matter what Mr Philips would like us to do to the contrary.

GTA V hits the right notes

Is there a more potent combination than high speed, danger and loud music? According to Rockstar and various reports in the gaming press, *GTA V* has the **most licensed songs in a GTA game** with 508 tracks. This includes the songs that were added exclusively to the Xbox One and PS4 releases of the game, as well as tunes included via *GTA Online* updates.

However, it's *GTA IV* with the **most radio stations in a**

GTA game. Including those that are featured in both *GTA IV* DLC expansions and the main game, *GTA IV* boasts a total of 23 individual stations, compared with 21 in *GTA V.*

First real-life celebrity to appear as themselves in a *GTA* game

Before the likes of comedian Ricky Gervais and film star Juliette Lewis made cameos in *GTA* games, musician Phil Collins appeared in 2006's *GTA: Vice City Stories* for the Sony PSP. The drummer and singer features in three missions, even playing an in-game concert.

Spills! Thrills! Headache pills!

A biker who choose a very odd place to dismbark after hitching a mid-flight ride on the wing of a private jet (pictured below)... A pimped-up golf cart being commndeered by Trevor Philips... An a beach buggy with a chimpnzee doing the driving... These are just a selection of the daring feats, painful-lookig flops and quirky glitches exposed in "AWESOME GTA 5 STUNTS & FAILS". Since being published

on YouTube on 16 Apr 2015, "RedKeyMon"'s nearly-17-min compilation has been the talk of Liberty City and beyond. The collection of clips from the king of crazy stunts had been viewed an astonishing 105,616,882 times as of 15 Feb 2019, the **most views for a GTA-related video**. One viewer commented: "This is and will always be the best video of *GTA* in history. I always come back to this video!"

FASTEST TIME TO EAT BIG SMOKE'S CLUCKIN' BELL MEAL

New record holder admits: "That was a lot of food"

In May 2017, competitive eater Matt Stonie (USA) recreated the infamous drive-thru food order in *GTA: San Andreas* by consuming a meal of equal calories in 34 min 52 sec. Since Cluck-

in' Bell doesn't exist in his city, Matt took the Big Smoke challenge by ordering equivalent meals at McDonald's and other restaurants. The YouTube video documenting Matt's feat had been viewed 17,974,703 times as of 14 Feb 2019. It's not been reported when, or even if, Matt ever felt hungry again...

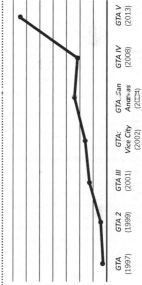

GTA MARKET PERFORMANCE CHART *Sponsored by PetsOvernight.com*

Since the landmark release of the first *Grand Theft Auto* (1997), the *GTA* franchise had sold more than 157 million copies as of 14 Feb 2019, according to VGChartz. *GTA V* heads the pack with 65.62 million sales. See our exclusive graphic for how that total breaks down for each main-series game released so far.

GTA (1997)	GTA 2 (1999)	GTA III (2001)	GTA: Vice City (2002)	GTA: San Andreas (2004)	GTA IV (2008)	GTA V (2013)

Y-axis: 0, 10, 20, 30, 40, 50, 60, 70

Black Cellphones

Need to upgrade your mobile? Just dial 1-999-367-3767

Our prices will blow your mind!

INSIDE

"I was a teenage werewolf"
The Beast speaks out at last

Bargain-basement Bigfoot
Does Sasquatch shop at Supa Save?

"I'll see them in court"
Lacey Jonas's star to be removed from the Vinewood Walk of Fame

PLUS...
GTA VI – coming to a console near you?

FORTNITE

Each year, we dedicate an entire chapter of the Gamer's Edition to a trending subject. Previously, this has included Star Wars and Minecraft, but this year there was only one real option: Fortnite!

FIRST PLAYER TO REACH 100,000 ELIMINATIONS

US pro gamer "HighDistortion" (aka Jimmy Moreno) left "Ninja", "nixxxay" and every other *Fortnite Battle Royale* player in the dust to reach this landmark elimination count first. Check out his Twitter feed from 21 Jan 2019 and you too can watch him notch up his 100,000th casualty on *Fortnite*'s island.

GUINNESS
WORLD RECORDS

FORTNITE

FIRST BATTLE ROYALE WITH 250 MILLION REGISTERED PLAYERS

On 20 Mar 2019, Epic Games confirmed that *Fortnite Battle Royale* had achieved 250 million registered players. The publisher rarely discloses its games' player counts, but reaching a quarter of a billion users was clearly something to shout about – especially with the rise of a contender to its battle-royale dominance in the shape of EA's *Apex Legends* – see pp.106–07 for more on that.

PHENOMENAL FORTNITE

"Phenomenal" really is the only word to use when trying to sum up *Fortnite*'s success. In just two years, the battle royale has been played by millions, becoming an everyday term and a streaming sensation.

THE STORM

The Storm is a force of health-sapping energy that slowly spreads across *Fortnite*'s map to force players into an ever-smaller area. Nobody knows where it came from, just that it's well worth steering clear of – so make sure you stay in its eye.

First game to support cross-play across Sony, Microsoft and Nintendo platforms

On 26 Sep 2018, *Fortnite* became the first game to allow cross-play on all major gaming platforms. This included Microsoft's Xbox One, the Nintendo Switch, PC, Android and iOS mobile devices, and, following a change of policy by Sony, the PS4. After earlier rejecting calls for cross-play, Sony finally gave in to demands from PlayStation owners and tested cross-play in an open public beta on the above date. Epic Games also created a means for gamers to merge any accounts they'd created on separate platforms. This meant that players could access skins, emotes and other unlockables, no matter where they'd purchased them.

383 PARTICIPANTS

On 28 Oct 2018, the *Fortnite* stand at Paris Games Week became a sea of pink. At the Expo Porte de Versailles exhibition complex in Paris, France, 383 people in Cuddle Team Leader hoodies set the record for the **most participants in a videogame emote routine**. The group danced for two minutes through a series of *Fortnite* moves, including the Floss, Best Mates, Take the L and the Hype. Leading the troupe was Dina Morisset, a French dance champion, who tweeted: "We made history."

Most concurrently played videogame

In Mar 2019, Epic Games Korea CEO Park Sung-chul confirmed that *Fortnite Battle Royale* had hit a peak of 10.8 million concurrent players. The landmark count is thought to have been set around the start of Season 8 (28 Feb 2019) and was even bigger than the 10 million-plus who watched DJ Marshmello's concert on 2 Feb 2019 (see pp.58–59). That huge player count can be attributed to the fact that the game is free to play and can be enjoyed on so many systems (see above). Judging by *Fortnite*'s huge number of registered players (250 million and rising), it's clear that it's also great fun to play.

Most watched *Fortnite*-themed YouTube video

As of 29 Apr 2019, "The Fortnite Rap Battle | #NerdOut ft Ninja, CDNThe3rd, Dakotaz, H2O Delirious & More" by "NerdOut!" had amassed 96,097,735 views since being uploaded to YouTube on 10 Mar 2018. The comedy *Fortnite*-themed rap features "Ninja" and over-the-top footage from the game.

FORTNITE

MOST VICTORY ROYALES IN FORTNITE BATTLE ROYALE

As of 30 Oct 2018, Brazilian gamer "ViniciusΔmazingシ" had the most Victory Royales across solo and team-based play. Having participated in 11,746 matches, the PS4 player had fought his way to 5,567 wins – giving him a victory rate of 47.40% to boot. His *Battle Royale* triumphs comprised 83 as a solo player, 112 in a duo and 5,372 in a four-player squad. Along the way, he also claimed 38,443 eliminations.

#1 VICTORY ROYALE

PLAYERS & PROS

No doubt you think you're pretty handy in a battle royale – but the players on these pages take it to another level. Prepare to meet the meanest and most deadly *Fortnite* players around...

Highest-earning *Fortnite Battle Royale* e-sports player

As of 12 Feb 2019, the USA's "Tfue" (aka Turner Tenney) had claimed $463,800 (£359,568) in *Fortnite* e-sports events. His biggest win was the $255,000 (£199,889) he scooped during 2018's "*Fortnite* Fall Skirmish Series – Week 6 – Grand Finals @ TwitchCon".

Longest *Fortnite* winning streaks

Croatia's "COOLER eXzacT" (left) had the **longest winning streak while playing solo**, as of 30 Oct 2018. The gamer fought his way to 36 consecutive wins. His streak was two more than the 34 consecutive wins chalked up by "NoPiicturesYT".

As of the same date, the **longest winning streak while playing as part of a squad** was achieved by "FeroX M33P_". Tactical team play and sublime skill saw "M33P_" claim 66 victories on the spin, with his total topping that of his squadmates "FeroX_TastyHero" and "FeroX Loyal" by just two. His is **the longest winning streak of any player**, whether playing solo or in a team.

Most Victory Royales in *Fortnite* (solo)

American "SoaR PierXBL" has claimed more victories as a solo player than any other *Fortnite* enthusiast. As of 13 Dec 2018, the lone wolf gamer had fought off other fellow solo players, duos and teams to claim victory on no fewer than 4,531 occasions, according to FortniteTracker. During his stint, the Xbox player clocked up a win rate of 46.23% across the 9,800 matches he played solo.

THE STORM

A coin toss was used to settle the 33rd qualifier at 2018's Fortnite Summer Skirmish qualifiers at PAX West, Seattle, USA. Grand Finals entry and $5,000 winnings were awarded to "The_Real_Cryohme at the expense of "SGG Colton".

Most eliminations in a single match of *Fortnite Battle Royale* (squad combined)

An Australian squad consisting of players "Fortitude_Fqrbes", "Nexjs", "tactjc-" and "TTV_NadeXC" eliminated a combined 61 players in a single Battle Royale on 8 Oct 2018. The squad members eliminated 25, 18, 10 and eight players respectively as they ran amok in Tilted Towers.

Most followed Twitch channel

As of 29 Apr 2019, American *Fortnite* player and broadcaster "Ninja" (aka Richard Tyler Blevins) had 14,064,046 followers on Twitch, according to SocialBlade. Twitch viewers have favoured his aggressive approach during rounds of *Fortnite*, with "Ninja" well known for prioritizing eliminations over Victory Royales. His popularity has led to him fronting major public events, including welcoming in 2019 during the "Ninja's Big New Year's Eve Stream" at Times Square, New York City, USA.

FORTNITE

LARGEST LEGO® BRICK *FORTNITE* WEAPON

Built by LEGO designer and YouTuber "ZaziNombies LEGO Creations" (aka Kyle L Neville, CAN), this scale replica of *Fortnite*'s Minigun was 140 cm (4 ft 7 in) long, used over 5,000 individual bricks and weighed more than 8 kg (17 lb 10 oz).

The giant weapon, first revealed on 22 Feb 2018 in a YouTube video, took "ZaziNombies" seven days to build, working eight (or more) hours per day, for a build time of over 60 hours! He used olive-green bricks as the weapon's main colour, while its blue power source was created using the satellite dish from an Arctic Explorers LEGO set.

Most popular *Fortnite* skin request

Few *Fortnite* skins have resonated with fans like the mighty Tender Defender (aka the Chicken Trooper). Created by eight-year-old Connor (above) and posted to Reddit by his father, "tfoust10", on 12 Sep 2018, the skin had earned more than 44,700 upvotes as of 31 Oct 2018. Epic answered the fans' calls by adding the Tender Defender to *Fortnite*'s item shop on 23 Nov 2018.

WEAPONS & SKINS

Winning Battle Royales is one thing, but for many players, looking the part is just as important. Here, we detail the skins and weapons that'll make you stand out from the rest.

First grappling gun in *Fortnite*

Added on 6 Sep 2018 in update 5.40, "The Grappler" was the first grappling gun for Epic's shooter. The weapon fires a suction cup that stays attached to the gun by a rope and sticks to walls. This lets skilled players quickly climb vertical structures, including defences built by other players, to get the drop on their unsuspecting rivals.

Choose your weapon (very carefully)

Dealing marginally more damage per second (DPS) than a feather duster, the **least damaging weapon in** *Fortnite* is the Rare Bolt-Action Sniper Rifle (1) at just 34.7 DPS. The Legendary Minigun (2), Legendary Double-Barrel Shotgun (3) and Rare Submachine Gun (4) are the **most damaging weapons per second**, each dealing 228 DPS.

The **most damaging weapon (single shot)** is the Legendary Heavy Sniper (5). According to FortniteTracker, it deals 157 damage per shot and is similarly deadly to scenery and structures.

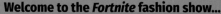

Welcome to the *Fortnite* fashion show...

The **first console-exclusive** *Fortnite* **skin** was the Blue Team Leader (1), released for the PS4 on 14 Feb 2018 to PS+ members. The **most expensive skin** is the Galaxy (2). It's available only to owners of Samsung's Galaxy Note 9 or Tab S4 devices, meaning you'll have to pay around $999 (£795) for it. The **rarest skin in** *Fortnite* was the Recon Expert (3) – the Season 1 skin was available only from 27 Oct to 12 Nov 2017. The Halloween-inspired Skull Trooper (4), from Oct 2017, was the **first holiday-themed skin**.

THE STORM

On 6 Aug 2018, "patricklaserguy" (aka Patrick Priebe, DEU) posted footage of his "working" Zapotron, based on *Fortnite*'s laser gun. The device took six weeks to build and, though it's hardly deadly, it can pop balloons from across a room.

FORTNITE

1 Season 1 (25 Oct–13 Dec 2017)

Although Season 1 didn't start until 25 Oct 2017, *Fortnite Battle Royale* went live on 26 Sep 2017. At that time, its map had just 10 named Points of Interest (POIs). Of those, only four – Pleasant Park, Retail Row, Fatal Fields and Lonely Lodge – remained as of 14 Mar 2019. These **longest-lasting POIs** had stood for 1 year 169 days.

8 Season 8 (28 Feb–8 May 2019)

As Season 7 ended, tremors were felt across the island. Season 8 began with a volcanic eruption that destroyed Wailing Woods and caused a jungle to cover the north-east of the island. Lazy Links was submerged under water, creating Lazy Lagoon. Finally, pirates invaded the island, prompting players to hunt for their hidden treasure.

THE BLOCK

1 PLEASANT PARK

5 LOOT LA

2 TILTED TOWERS

GLOOMY GOALS

SNOBBY SHORES

4

VIKING VILLAGE

A MAP FOR ALL SEASONS

Eight seasons of *Fortnite* (as of 8 May 2019) have kept millions of players very busy. At the centre of all that entertainment is the game's famous map – an ever-shifting landscape that ushers in new areas and rewarding challenges...

FROSTY FLIGHTS

WACKY WORKSHOP

HAPPY HAMLET

7

7 Season 7 (6 Dec 2018–27 Feb 2019)

A gigantic iceberg hit the island, covering a huge area in ice and creating Happy Hamlet, Frosty Flights and Polar Peak. Season 7 brought the game's **first plane** (the X-4 Stormwing) and (briefly) its **first sword** – the Infinity Blade. On 2 Feb, Marshmello hosted the **largest music concert in a game**, with more than 10 million players partying (right).

6

2 Season 2
(14 Dec 2017–21 Feb 2018)

With the launch of Season 2, the game took a big step towards the *Fortnite* we know today by introducing the Battle Pass. It offered 70 tiers of rewards and an additional daily challenge. It also ushered in a medieval theme and changed the map with the appearance of Tilted Towers, Shifty Shafts, Haunted Hills, Junk Junction and Snobby Shores.

3 Season 3
(22 Feb–30 Apr 2018)

Millions of players were amazed when Season 3's space theme brought with it a gigantic meteor that threatened to reduce one of *Fortnite*'s locations to rubble. Sure enough, when the meteor hit (just as Season 3 turned to Season 4), the area known as Dusty Depot was obliterated and the impact crater renamed as Dusty Divot.

4 Season 4
(1 May–11 Jul 2018)

Shortly after the meteor hit, Thanos made an appearance – the **first Marvel character in *Fortnite***. Once he'd left, a rocket blasted off from Snobby Shores – the **first live in-game event to occur simultaneously across six platforms**. Players were able to watch on PS4, Xbox One, Switch, PC, iOS and Android as the rocket opened a time rift.

5 Season 5
(12 Jul–26 Sep 2018)

After the rocket launch, Adobe Village appeared and Tomato Temple time-warped to the present day to replace Tomato Town. Climate change also caused Moisty Mire to turn to desert, as Paradise Palms was born. Stranger still, The Cube (aka Kevin, right) emerged from the rift in the sky and dissolved into the waters of Loot Lake.

6 Season 6
(27 Sep–5 Dec 2018)

The Cube re-emerged, attaching itself to Loot Lake's island, then carrying itself, and the island, into the air. Eventually, The Cube and the island exploded, triggering the Halloween-themed "Fortnitemares" event on 24 Oct – *Fortnite*'s **first PvE event**. Players fought back the tides of Cube Monsters while still contending with each other.

"ROCKYNOHANDS" Q&A

A serious fall in 2006 left Rocky Stoutenburgh (aka "RockyNoHands") paralysed from the neck down. Despite this, he trained himself over many years to play games via a mouth-operated controller. He now regularly streams his Fortnite exploits on his Twitch channel.

Most Victory Royales in *Fortnite* using a QuadStick mouth-operated joystick

As of 26 Mar 2019, "RockyNoHands" had fought his way to 509 *Fortnite* Victory Royales using a QuadStick, as verified by FortniteTracker. The US gamer had also eliminated 11 rival players in a single game – the **most eliminations in a match of *Fortnite Battle Royale* using a QuadStick**.

Q&A

We spoke to "RockyNoHands" in late 2018. Go to **www.guinnessworldrecords.com/gamers** to watch our full video interview with him.

How were you after the accident?
The future seemed bleak. I lost my job. Soon after, all my friends disappeared or showed their true colours. I spent a lot of time doing nothing. [But] family is everything. Friends come and go, but family is for ever.

Did gaming help?
I was watching my brother play Xbox a lot. Then he found the QuadStick online and told me I should try it out. Eventually I bought one, then never looked back. It's awesome. You always have people to game with [or] talk to.

How does the QuadStick work?
It has a joystick, four sip/puff pressure sensors and a lip-position sensor, which is able to be assigned to output to any controller button, a mouse or to a keyboard key.

Was it difficult at first?
[It's] trial and error, practice. Every game starts out rough until you learn your limitations. It's a lot at first remembering all the buttons for each action, especially if you play multiple games.

What games do you play most?
Pretty much anything I see interesting or challenging: *Fortnite*, *PUBG*, *Rocket League*, *WoW*, *For Honor*, *Call of Duty: Black Ops 4*, *NHL*. I was a high-level *For Honor* player on Xbox.

How does it feel to have a GWR title and an appearance in the *Gamer's* book?
It means a lot. I've always been interested in world records. Then I got paralysed and dreams faded. So it feels damn good to be a two-time record holder and once again show the world if there's a will there's a way. I can't wait till I get the *Gamer's Edition* for my nephew John Hamilton and see if he notices [that I'm in it]!

What do you say to people who see their disability as a barrier to gaming?
Just try it. I was horrible at gaming when I first started. Start small, build up to bigger and better. If a guy can play games with his mouth better than most people, then I'm sure everyone has a shot at their goals.

FORTNITE

Creator: ITSCIZZORZ
Course name: CizzorzDeathRun Challenge
Island code: 0940-9970-7913

Deadliest Deathruns

Traps, traps and more traps! Spikes shooting out of walls, fiery-hot lava pooling on the floor and electrified ceilings are just the start of the fiendish ways you might come a cropper in one of these constructions. The best deathruns require skill and dexterity to survive, but the important thing is that each room in your course must have a possible escape route.

CREATIVE MODE CHALLENGES

Creative Mode is a game-changer in the most literal sense, as you can use its building tools to craft challenges for others to attempt. Read on to find out how your creations could be used in future record attempts...

HOW TO APPLY

The Fortnite Readers' Challenge section of our website has all the information you need to submit your designs. Visit www.guinnessworldrecords.com/gamers, making sure you have your Island code to hand, as well as a brief description of your course. We'll get in touch should we choose your course for a record attempt.

ON YOUR MARKS, GET SET, CREATE!

How would you like to have your *Fortnite* creation become part of a Guinness World Records attempt? Here at GWR HQ, we're looking to find players who've mastered *Fortnite*'s Creative Mode so we can use their deathruns, parkour courses, mazes and racetracks in our records. If you possess the skills and like the idea of having other players try to set the fastest times in your creation, then we want to hear from you (see "How to apply", right). And if you need inspiration, we've included the Island codes for some of the most popular examples from each type of challenge.

We'll also be showcasing the best courses submitted on our YouTube channel, so the world can see your amazing constructions!

GUINNESS
WORLD RECORDS

Creator: JXDVN

Course name:
Adventures in Wonderland Part 1

Island code: 2611-2622-9927

Creator: WERTANDREW

Course name:
Apa Parkour University

Island code: 9469-8901-1491

A-maze-ing Mazes

Whether it's a traditional hedge maze or a labyrinth made from wood or stone – or whatever else takes your fancy – the only limit to the mazes you construct is your own imagination. We're looking for mazes that will have players running around in circles.

Punishing Parkour

A parkour – or freerunning – course should be the ultimate test of speed, strength and poise for the people who attempt them. Your stage should have players springing from ledge to ledge, leaping to moving platforms and trying to time their jumps perfectly to blast off Shockwave Grenade detonations.

Creator: MOMMA_MAK

Course name:
Momma Mak's Paradise Isle

Island code: 7489-2231-7837

Trickiest Tracks

Racing is one of *Fortnite*'s most exciting activities, and it just so happens that laying out your own racetrack is lots of fun as well. You're even able to select the vehicles that players can use on your course. And, naturally, you're free to make its setting as fantastical as you like.

REALM ROYALE

BLACKOUT

FIRESTORM

Highest level player in *Realm Royale*

German gamer "handwerk3r ttv btw" has fought his way through the player levels in Hi-Rez Studios' *Realm Royale* (2018). As of 28 Mar 2019, the gamer had reached level 83 in the free-to-play offshoot of *Paladins: Champions of the Realm* (2018). In 5,409 games, the PC player had racked up an impressive 1,231 wins, according to statistics from the RealmTracker website. That's an overall victory ratio of 22.8%.

Most wins in *Call of Duty: Black Ops 4 Blackout*

As of 28 Mar 2019, "bobbypoff_" (aka Bobby Poffenbarger) ranked first in two of the main categories in *Blackout*, the battle-royale mode in Activision's *Call of Duty: Black Ops 4* (2018). The American had 1,725 wins to his name from a total of 5,708 engagements. He had also racked up 30,268 kills in the battle royale – the **most kills in Blackout**. In short, if you see him coming – RUN!

First battle-royale mode in the *Battlefield* series

When EA released *Battlefield V* on 20 Nov 2018, the much-anticipated battle-royale mode was AWOL. Players had to wait until 25 Mar 2019 to get their hands on *Firestorm*. In the end, the new addition turned out to be a 64-player, team-based shooter in which players are broken up into four-person squads. Vehicles play a key part – this is a *Battlefield* game, after all – while the *Firestorm* itself is the name given to the fiery cyclone that engulfs the map.

LAST BATTLE

"Ten-hut!" What you have before you is a collection of the most popular battle-royale games the world has ever seen! From the veterans to the new recruits, we put the best examples of the genre through their paces.

APEX LEGENDS

Fastest-growing battle-royale game

Within just three days of its launch on 4 Feb 2019, *Apex Legends* (EA) had notched up 10 million registered players. That meant its growth was even swifter than the mighty *Fortnite*, which took two weeks to reach the same milestone in Oct 2017. *Apex*'s expansion didn't halt there, either (see pp.106–07). In the fast-paced game, 60 players in teams of three pick a Legend and do their best to survive.

Most Twitch channels for a videogame

It seems that watching *Fortnite* (Epic, 2017) is almost as addictive as playing it. As of 29 Mar 2019, the game had been live-streamed on a huge 66,600 Twitch channels. The next most popular game was *Apex Legends*, but even EA's in-vogue battle royale had been streamed on *only* 18,919 channels.

PUBG

Most concurrent players on Steam for a videogame

As of 23 Apr 2019, the game on Steam with most players at the same time was *PLAYERUNKNOWN'S BATTLEGROUNDS* (PUBG Corporation, 2017). It was on 13 Jan 2018 that the game recorded an all-time peak of 3,257,248 players. The astonishing figure was reached at the height of *PUBG*'s popularity and confirmed at www.steamdb.info. It's worth noting that neither *Fortnite* nor *Apex Legends* is available on Steam.

FORTNITE

ROYALE STANDING

ADVENTURERS

Pick up your sword, grab your shield and dust off your best leather tunic – it's time to go adventuring. For the brave characters in this chapter, no task is too arduous, no journey too far and no villain too tough.

Most PlayStation Platinum trophies won

Not one to shirk the call of an adventure, Bahraini gamer Hakam Karim – more commonly known as "Hakoom" – has dedicated a sizeable chunk of his life to completing as many PlayStation games as possible. As of 12 Feb 2019, he had acquired a remarkable 1,857 PlayStation Platinum trophies, as verified by PSNProfiles – adding to his tally since we awarded him a GWR record certificate (below) in Sep 2018. He told us his aim was to make "my friends and family and country proud of me". Job done. But he hasn't stopped there. He also has the **most PlayStation trophies** – accumulating 74,243 Bronze, Silver, Gold and Platinum trophies.

GUINNESS WORLD RECORDS

CERTIFICATE

The most PlayStation platinum trophies won by an individual is 1,691, achieved by Hakam Karim aka Hakoom (Bahrain) as verified on 19 September 2018.

OFFICIALLY AMAZING

RECORD HOLDER

UNCHARTED A Thief's End
RESIDENT EVIL biohazard
PERSONA 5
UNCHARTED DRAKE'S DECEPTION
THE LAST OF US REMASTERED
UNCHARTED DRAKE'S FORTUNE
MONSTER HUNTER WORLD
SPIDER-MAN
THE LAST OF US
PORTAL 2
METAL GEAR SOLID 4 GUNS OF THE PATRIOTS

COMING UP ▸▸▸

LINK

The Legend of Zelda's green-clad, sword-wielding hero has long since become a legend in his own right. His amazing adventures rank among Nintendo's – and therefore gaming's – best-ever titles.

Largest Labo vehicle peripheral

Breath of the Wild's "The Champions' Ballad" DLC provided Link with a new ride in the shape of the Master Cycle Zero. The rune-powered motorcycle was recreated by Australia's Jordan Booth, who built his version out of cardboard. It measured 1.77 m (5 ft 9 in) long and he even made it Labo-compatible so he could use it to control *Mario Kart 8 Deluxe* (Nintendo, 2017)! He unveiled his creation on YouTube on 4 Sep 2018.

Most expensive *Legend of Zelda* game

On 16 Jan 2019, more than 30 collectors pursued a fully boxed and factory-sealed copy of Nintendo's vintage NES adventure *The Legend of Zelda* (1986). The wrapped Classic Series edition ultimately sold for $3,360 (£2,614) on Heritage Auctions' website.

Most ubiquitous action-adventure videogame character

Including *Super Smash Bros. Ultimate* (Nintendo, 2018), Link has featured in 40 unique games. Away from the core *Zelda* games, his noteworthy appearances include *Mario Kart 8,* three Philips CD-i titles and Sega's *Sonic Lost World*.

Longest time to discover a new *Super Smash Bros. Melee* technique

On 21 Oct 2018, 16 years 334 days after the release of *Super Smash Bros. Melee* (Nintendo, 2001), Link main "Savestate" (aka Joseph El-Khouri) took to Twitter to demonstrate a new technique. Coined "The Bomb Rocket", it involved using Link's bombs to blast off into the air.

Fastest completion of *The Legend of Zelda: Skyward Sword*

US gamer "Nimzo" paid little heed to any sidequests found in the 2011 adventure, flying through it in 4 hr 50 min 59 sec on 14 Aug 2018, as verified by Speedrun. "I still want to lower this time," stated the record holder.

WEAPON SELECT

Almost as well known as Link is his assortment of magical weapons and items. Here, we list Link's must-have kit from 1986's *The Legend of Zelda*.

Magical Sword

Magical Shield

Bow and Arrow

Bomb

Recorder

Boomerang

Power Bracelet

Magical Rod

MOST CRITICALLY ACCLAIMED PLAYABLE CHARACTER

With six unique entries in the top 100 of GameRankings' best-reviewed games as of 6 Mar 2019, Link enjoys the most critical acclaim of any lead protagonist. Ranked by highest score, Link's six top-rated *Legend of Zelda* titles are 1998's *Ocarina of Time* (97.54%, N64); 2017's *Breath of the Wild* (97.33%, Switch); 2006's Wii title *Twilight Princess* (94.58%); 2002's *The Wind Waker* (94.43%, GameCube); 2011's *Ocarina of Time 3D* (93.89%, 3DS); and 2011's *Skyward Sword* (93.15%, Wii). Link even leaves fellow Nintendo star Mario trailing in his critically acclaimed dust.

THE LEGEND OF ZELDA
25th ANNIVERSARY

NEMESIS

As the third component of *Zelda*'s magical Triforce, Ganondorf is as evil as Link and Princess Zelda are good. He can even take on the form of a monstrous boar known as Ganon as he tries to reduce the kingdom of Hyrule to ruin.

NEXT APPEARANCE

Some 26 years after Link washed up on the shores of Koholint Island in *Link's Awakening* for the Game Boy, he's about to do it all over again. Nintendo revealed a charming-looking Switch remake during a Feb 2019 Direct.

MASTER CHIEF

It's deeds not words that define *Halo*'s enigmatic supersoldier. Who has time for talk when human civilization itself is at stake? The Spartan has been saving us from extermination since 2001, and yet he doesn't look a day older (possibly because we've yet to see his face)...

LOVE STORY

Can romance blossom between an AI construct with no physical form and a battle-hardened warrior? That's not an existential question, but a topic of debate among *Halo* fans. The most popular theory is that Cortana and the Chief do love each other, just not in the romantic sense.

First *Halo* arcade game

Released in selected Dave & Buster's locations in the USA and Canada in Jul 2018, *Halo: Fireteam Raven* was the first arcade game based on the franchise. The light-gun game recreates some of the locations from *Halo: Combat Evolved* (2001). Players assume control of Orbital Drop Shock Troopers (ODST), who fight alongside Master Chief against Covenant forces and the Flood.

Highest Xbox Live GamerScore

On 21 Nov 2018, Xbox devotee "Stallion83" (aka Raymond Cox, USA) finally saw his record haul of Xbox GamerScore points reach two million. Ray was playing *Halo 2* (from *Halo: The Master Chief Collection*) at the magic moment, which he broadcast live on Twitch. He even planned it so that the achievements that took his score to two million were those unlocked upon completing the game.

NEXT APPEARANCE

Microsoft opened its E3 2018 showcase with the grand unveiling of *Halo Infinite*. The trailer put the spotlight on the gorgeous environments generated by the new Slipspace engine – let's hope that the Chief has time to admire them between gunfights.

Most critically acclaimed shooter on Xbox

Halo: Combat Evolved – released for the original Xbox console back in 2001 – introduced us to the Master Chief, but it was equally memorable for its open-ended, innovative gameplay. Its mighty GameRankings score of 95.54% – averaged out from 78 reviews – still blows a hole in any other Xbox shooter, *Halo*-derived or otherwise. One of its many rave reviews called it a "showstopper".

70

WEAPON SELECT

No matter if he's fighting Covenant, Prometheans or the Flood, the Chief needs all the help he can get. It's a good job that the UNSC provides lethal hardware to its soldiers.

Pistol

The go-to gun for true connoisseurs of *Halo: Combat Evolved*.

Assault Rifle

Lacks power, but makes up for it with a rapid rate of fire.

M90 Shotgun

The ideal weapon for those all-too-close encounters.

Sniper Rifle

Perfect for picking off bad guys from a discreet distance.

Rocket Launcher

Covenant tank standing in your way? Give it a rocket...

Frag Grenade

Enemies behind cover? One of these will flush them out.

BEST-SELLING SCI-FI SHOOTER VIDEOGAME SERIES

Halo's first-person shooters had racked up global sales of 65.08 million as of 8 Feb 2019, according to VGChartz. The best-selling game in the series' history is 2007's *Halo 3*, with 12.13 million physical copies sold. Prequel *Halo: Reach* (2010, 9.97 million) and *Halo 4* (2012, 9.96 million) were the next highest sellers. The franchise is light years ahead of shooters by other sci-fi heavyweights, including *Star Wars*, *Killzone* and *Half-Life*.

$639,125

As of 7 Feb 2019, the USA's "Lethul" (aka Tony Campbell) was the **highest-earning** *Halo* **player**. According to Esportsearnings, he'd won $639,125 (£493,461), including $250,000 at the 2016 World Championship and $30,000 at DreamHack Atlanta on 18 Nov 2018.

MONSTER HUNTERS

Capcom's *Monster Hunter* series has demonstrated that bigger is better for over 15 years. But as jaw-dropping as its enormous beasts are, the series wouldn't be anywhere without its humble, sword-swinging, BBQ-grilling behemoth hunters.

SNAPSHOT

Usually, it's the monster hunters who are the ones dealing out damage to the many savage beasts of the land. But in *MHW*, the monsters are just as likely to be scrapping among themselves. The game's living, breathing world was a significant step forward for the franchise. It made for some amazing in-game moments as its monsters squared off against each other, teeth and claws at the ready.

Fastest completion of "The White Winds of the New World" quest in *Monster Hunter World* (*MHW*)

"The White Winds of the New World" is often cited as the 2018 game's hardest quest, but it held few fears for "Jinfurai". The US speedster completed it in 6 min 23 sec, as verified on 13 Sep 2018 by Speedrun. The quest gives gamers a tight time limit of 25 min to overcome several fierce beasts, including a Legiana, Odogaron, Diablos and Rathalos (above).

WEAPON SELECT

There's a weapon to suit just about everybody's style in *MHW* – from hammers that let you bash the very scales off your prey to swords sharp enough to pierce even the toughest hide. Here are some of the weapon types that we favour in the heat of battle.

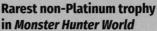
Sword and Shield | Dual Blades | Long Sword

NEXT APPEARANCE

The hunters got so good at their job that some beasts elected to take flight! Don't worry: you can follow them when the *MHW: Iceborne* expansion is released in late 2019.

Rarest non-Platinum trophy in *Monster Hunter World*

As of 5 Mar 2019, only 1.2% of PS4 players had unlocked the "Giant Crown Master" trophy, according to PSNProfiles. To get it, players must obtain a gold crown (earned when defeating especially large monsters) for almost every species that is listed in their hunting log.

MOST CRITICALLY ACCLAIMED *MONSTER HUNTER* GAME

Monster Hunter games are often well received by critics, with many of them averaging 80% and above on GameRankings. But it's the PS4 version of Capcom's 2018 hit *Monster Hunter World* that sits at the top of the food chain. As of 5 Mar 2019, it enjoyed an average score of 89.71% across 51 reviews. One reviewer called it "impossible not to love", going on to say that it's one of a "few games in recent memory that feels so satisfying to play".

| Gunlance | Heavy Bowgun | Switch Axe | Hunting Horn | Insect Glaive |

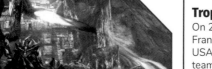

93 MONSTERS

Monster Hunter Generations Ultimate (Capcom, 2018) has the **franchise's largest monster count**. In all, the Switch game includes 93 formidable beasts, including the never-before-seen silver-scaled Valstrax (above).

Trophy hunters

On 28 Jul 2018, in San Francisco, California, USA, Social Dissonance team members "Sam" (on the left) and "Shepard" (right) of the USA became the **first winners of the *Monster Hunter World* USA Championship**. They used Switch Axes to take down a fearsome Nergigante in 3 min 3 sec.

ALOY

Life is tough in the ravaged futuristic version of Earth in *Horizon Zero Dawn* (Sony, 2017), but then so is Aloy. With just one adventure under her belt, she has already sealed her place as a gaming great.

SNAPSHOT 📷

Few *Horizon* players will forget the moment that Rost – Aloy's teacher and father figure – allows her to go face-to-serrated-spikes with a Sawtooth, one of the early game's most deadly monsters.

Most-destroyed machine in *Horizon Zero Dawn*

Watchers are the sentinels of *Horizon*'s world, ever vigilant for humans to terminate. This aggression has made them a regular target for Aloy and her trusty spear. *Horizon*'s player base had destroyed 1.8 billion of the machines as of 7 Mar 2018. Nearly three times as many Watchers had been bumped off than the next most-targeted machine, the Scrapper. It's *almost* enough to make you feel sorry for them.

Aloy's most-used trap

Aloy sets traps to snare and weaken the huge beasts that roam the land. Of all these traps, she's made most use of the Tripcaster. As of 7 Mar 2018, players had successfully deployed the trap 24.2 million times, according to Sony.

WEAPON SELECT

If you're going to brave *Horizon*'s sci-fi wilderness, it's best to go in prepared. As you'll see, Aloy has a host of deadly weaponry at her disposal. Just remember to use her Focus in order to scan the land's ferocious monsters for weak spots.

Spear
Your basic weapon. More effective than it may look.

War Bow
Picks off light-armoured foes from a safe distance.

Rattler
Targets have to dodge not just one bolt but five.

Hacking a ride

The vast landscapes of Aloy's world make taming a trusty steed a priority. The horse-like Strider had been overridden on 57.5 million occasions as of 7 Mar 2018, making it the **most-overridden machine in *Horizon*.** The fact that more Striders than Watchers have been overridden shows that players favour speed over protection.

Largest LEGO® brick *Horizon Zero Dawn* custom model

Marius Herrmann (DEU) had created LEGO models from *Titanfall* and *Halo*. He then turned to *Horizon*'s fearsome Thunderjaw, building a 65-cm (25.6-in) long model. The art director at Guerrilla Games (*Horizon*'s developer) called it "fantastic".

BEST-SELLING GAME STARRING A FEMALE LEAD

Aloy's combination of strength, skill and bravery has inspired gamers to buy *Horizon Zero Dawn* in their millions. Her debut, released on 28 Feb 2017, had sold an estimated nine million copies as of 28 Nov 2018, according to VGChartz. Of those, 5.38 million were retail copies and the remainder digital purchases. These sales figures tower over those of *Tomb Raider II* (Eidos, 1997), which was Lara Croft's best-selling game at 5.24 million copies sold, and the 5.36 million copies shifted of *Final Fantasy XIII* (Square Enix, 2009), which starred Lightning.

Use this to tie down the opposition.

Ropecaster

Forgefire

Turns up the heat by giving your enemies a very warm welcome.

Keep shooting – the damage by each bolt increases as you fire.

Stormslinger

Tearblaster

Capable of stripping away the metal armour of any foe.

Icy weapon that freezes attackers in their tracks.

Icerail

359.5 MILLION

Of all the vast arsenal of weaponry placed at Aloy's disposal (see the fearsome selection in the Weapon Select bar above), it's still her humble bow that players have used the most. Statistics issued by Sony in Mar 2018 showed that Aloy had fired 359.5 million arrows, making it the game's **most-fired weapon**. It's almost 300 million more than the next most-used weapon – that being the 61.7 million bombs hurled using her sling. Both dwarf the Icerail in usage, with the "Frozen Wilds" DLC weapon being wielded just 668,000 times.

75

SIMON BELMONT

Castlevania's vampire hunter has made it his life's work to hunt down the undead. The adventures of Simon – and of the rest of his Belmont kin – have raised the stakes for platformers.

NEMESIS 💀

Count Dracula never seems to tire of his onslaught against humanity. So much so that, despite being repeatedly defeated by Simon and other Belmonts, he's never more than a reincarnation away from wreaking havoc once more.

First Konami character to debut in a TV show

With a bottomless backpack and a sentient whip, Simon Belmont was part of the N-Team in *Captain N: The Game Master*. The cartoon series ran on US TV between 1989 and 1991. Fans argued he was barely recognisable. What do you reckon?

Most ubiquitous *Castlevania* hero

Simon (above centre) is the most recurring hero across *Castlevania*'s 27 titles. As of 18 Feb 2019, he'd topped the bill six times, putting him clear of Richter Belmont (top left) and Christopher Belmont (top right), who had three appearances each. In all, eight Belmonts have featured in the franchise's titles.

POWER-UP

Taking on the undead is not a task for the faint of heart. It also requires some unusual equipment. As you can see, Simon was well kitted out for the original 1987 NES *Castlevania*. Just about all he lacked was a string of garlic as he entered Dracula's castle.

Whip	**Dagger**	**Throwing Axe**
The Belmonts' deadly family heirloom.	Throwable blade that travels in straight lines.	Effective, but a tricky weapon to master.

First console game to be re-released as an arcade game

Arcade games often come to consoles. But the first one to make the trip the other way was Konami's *Haunted Castle* (1988) – a spin-off from *Castlevania*.

Fastest "Normal" completion of *Castlevania*

On 17 Mar 2019, American speedster "2_snek" drove Dracula's undead army from the classic 1987 NES game back to the Pit in just 11 min 27.33 sec. Commenting on Speedrun, the elated new record holder commented: "This was an awesome journey."

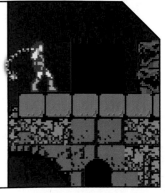

LONGEST REACH IN *SUPER SMASH BROS. ULTIMATE*

For fighting games that are contested at the highest levels, any advantage is precious. In *Super Smash Bros. Ultimate* (2018), Simon's edge is that his whip has the longest average reach among all characters in Nintendo's game. This makes Simon (and his "Echo" character Richter) a terrific zoning asset. As a result, he is able to keep his rivals at arm's length (well, whip's length) while still causing damage. His whip can extend to a range of four in-game units (the width of four average-sized characters).

Holy Water	Boomerang	Stopwatch	Cross	Invisibility Potion
Makes your foes go up in flames.	A faithful servant that always returns.	Freezes time for 5 sec, but use it wisely.	Clears a screen of enemies in quick time.	Does what it says on the tin, err, jug.

LOVE STORY

In one of the gaming world's first in-play relationships, Simon Belmont and Selena were married at the start of 1988 coin-op *Haunted Castle*. But the happy-ever-after didn't last long. Count Dracula soon kidnaps Simon's new wife, setting the groom on the path to rescue his bride from Dracula's cold clutches.

First fighting game to star Simon Belmont

Years before Simon graced *Super Smash Bros. Ultimate* for Switch, the vampire hunter was fighting his way through *DreamMix TV World Fighters* (Konami, 2003). The Japan-exclusive brawler starred characters from across many franchises, including Bomberman, Solid Snake and Optimus Prime.

77

KRATOS

The God of War might just be the angriest character you will meet in this book. But then, with family tragedy looming large over his past, who can blame him? Let's just hope that his 2018 outing has paved the way for a soothing of his soul.

Most deadly *GoW* boss

Kratos has fought many gods and monsters on his travels, but few are as ferocious as Sigrun, Queen of the Valkyries from *God of War* (2018). On the "Give Me God of War" difficulty setting, the killer queen fells players at a rate of 100:1!

Best-selling *God of War* videogame

Kratos's descent into Norse mythology in *God of War* (2018) is his top-selling game. As of 12 Feb 2019, his adventure had sold 6.15 million copies, according to VGChartz.

Largest land-based videogame boss

Cronos crashed into 2010's *God of War III* in a truly big way. Kratos literally climbs the Titan as they fight in one of his most memorable encounters. Estimates of Cronos's height vary hugely, from a "mere" 5,500 ft (1,676 m) to as much as 29,000 ft (8,839 m)!

WEAPON SELECT

Though the Blades of Chaos are Kratos's mainstay, he's not against picking up other arms when the opportunity arises – often as they're prised from the cold, dead hands of his latest victim. Here are some of our favourites.

Blades of Chaos	Blade of Artemis	Barbarian Hammer
God of War (2005)	*God of War* (2005)	*God of War II* (2007)

NEMESIS 💀

Kratos's thirst for revenge is such that even Zeus, father of the gods, is in his firing line. The encounter between father and son in *God of War III* marks the end of Kratos's battle through Olympus, but not the end of his odyssey.

28 MIN 12 SEC

Playing *God of War* (2018) on "Give Me a Story" difficulty makes slaying the nine Valkyries easier, but for speed-runners the real challenge is in finding the quickest path. The **fastest time to beat all nine Valkyries** was achieved by "Clowned187" (USA) on 5 Jul 2018, as verified by Speedrun.

MOST CRITICALLY ACCLAIMED HACK-AND-SLASH VIDEOGAME

Sony's *God of War* (2018) stands proudly as the best-reviewed hack-and-slash game ever. No wonder Kratos feels like he has something to shout about! The PS4 exclusive pits Kratos against the might of the Norse gods, but it was the dialogue between him and his son, Atreus, that earned the game its real plaudits. As of 12 Feb 2019, it had an aggregate GameRankings review score of 94.10%, averaged from 63 reviews. The title also earned a host of Game of the Year awards (see pp.12–13).

Spear of Destiny	Nemean Cestus	Claws of Hades	Arms of Sparta	Leviathan Axe

God of War II (2007)	*God of War III* (2010)	*God of War III* (2010)	*God of War: Ghost of Sparta* (2010)	*God of War* (2018)

SNAPSHOT 📷

Tricked into slaying his wife and daughter, the devastated Kratos is cursed to have the ashes of his dead family fused with his skin, never to be removed. His whitened flesh earns him the *nom de guerre* the "Ghost of Sparta". From this point on, Kratos's grief fuels his rage and his all-consuming desire to take bloody revenge on the Greek gods.

First high-definition remastering of a PS2 game

High-definition remasters of older games feel like a common occurrence these days, but the trend was started by Kratos's titles. The *God of War Collection* that launched on 17 Nov 2009 for the PS3 included HD remasters of his first two PS2 outings.

79

NATHAN DRAKE

Whether it's his easy-going nature, his wit or his ability to take on all-comers in a punch-up, Nathan Drake has proven to be one of gaming's most beloved characters. Of course, it also helps that he's the star of some of the best adventure games ever!

SNAPSHOT

You won't find an *Uncharted* game without a jaw-dropping set piece. But surely the most spectacular happens at the beginning of *Uncharted 2*, as a wounded Drake climbs up a train wreck that's dangling over a chasm!

Best-selling remastered videogame collection

Uncharted: The Nathan Drake Collection is the remaster of Nathan Drake's first trio of *Uncharted* games. Each game has gained improved graphics, new trophies and a photo mode – and it has proven a hit. As of 8 Oct 2018, the PS4 title had sold 5.55 million physical copies, according to VGChartz.

Fastest completion of *Uncharted 4: Survival*

On 3 Sep 2017, "LEANDER_GE" (DEU) successfully took on all 50 waves of enemies in *Uncharted 4: Survival* in 1 hr 27 min 37 sec. As verified by Speedrun, the survivor withstood the onslaught of soldiers, mercenaries and even ghost pirates (right) in *Uncharted 4*'s free expansion.

BOSS FIGHT

The *Uncharted* heroes have fought more than their fair share of villains on their travels. Here, we profile the "best" bad guys to feature in Naughty Dog's series.

Drake's Fortune (2007)
Atoq Navarro
A crooked archaeologist obsessed with gold.

Zoran Lazarević
Merciless, mad and almost invincible.

Among Thieves (2009)

Golden Abyss (2011)
Jason Dante
He'll cross anyone for enough cash.

Rarest *Uncharted* series Platinum trophy

If only it was as easy as in our image (right) to bag an *Uncharted* Platinum trophy! According to PSNProfiles, the rarest was that of *Uncharted 4: A Thief's End*, with just 0.8% of players claiming its Platinum as of 8 Oct 2018. *Uncharted: Drake's Fortune* had the **most-earned Platinum** at 3.4%.

LOVE STORY

LOVE-O-METER

The romantic journey that Elena Fisher and Nathan Drake go on is every bit as dramatic as any of their adventures. Elena's always there to help when Drake's in a spot of bother, and she's more than able to hold her own when the only option remaining is to fight.

96.43%

MOST CRITICALLY ACCLAIMED PLAYSTATION-EXCLUSIVE ACTION-ADVENTURE GAME

Drake's second outing, *Uncharted 2: Among Thieves*, is the top dog when it comes to exclusive action-adventures on PlayStation. Released on 13 Oct 2009, the Sony title wowed critics, scoring an average of 96.43% across 82 reviews, as verified by GameRankings. None of the later *Uncharted* games, nor *The Last of Us* (Sony, 2013) and *Horizon Zero Dawn* (Sony, 2017), has topped its average review score.

GUINNESS WORLD RECORDS®

Talbot
Written as the anti-Drake, this secretive agent is deadly.

Drake's Deception (2011)

A Thief's End (2016)

Rafe Adler
Rich through inheritance, he'll stop at nothing to build his own fortune.

Asav
A doctor-turned-warlord, out to free his country.

The Lost Legacy (2017)

First bullet wound suffered by Nathan Drake in *Uncharted*

According to a tweet sent by Naughty Dog's Jonathan Cooper on 8 Jul 2018, "Drake doesn't ever take bullet damage. The red UI that shows 'hits' is to represent his 'luck' running out." Therefore Drake has suffered only one bullet wound – from a shot fired in an *Uncharted 2* cutscene.

4,307,941 VIEWS

Directed by Allan Ungar and starring Nathan Fillion as Nathan Drake, "*Uncharted* – Live Action Fan Film (2018)" was the **most viewed fan film based on *Uncharted*** as of 31 Aug 2018. In the film, first uploaded to YouTube on 16 Jul 2018, a typically wisecracking Drake is captured by drug barons.

81

LARA CROFT

Action-archaeologist Lara Croft is the best-known female protagonist in videogames. These days, she's a trailblazer as well, with *Horizon Zero Dawn*'s Aloy (pp.74–75), *The Last of Us*'s Ellie (pp.118–19) and plenty more female adventurers following her lead.

NEMESIS

Not one enemy for Lara but many. Trinity is a secret organization that seeks the power of ancient artefacts for its own designs. Lara and her father, Richard James Croft, are both in the organization's bad books.

2 HR 54 MIN 14 SEC

Croft's latest adventure is rich with secrets to discover, but for those who want a greater challenge, there's always the game's speed-run to contest. The **fastest completion of *Shadow of the Tomb Raider*** (Square Enix, 2018) was achieved by PC player "D3kker" (NLD), who took 2 hr 54 min 14 sec, as verified by Speedrun on 23 Dec 2018.

SNAPSHOT 📷

Lara Croft knew to expect trouble in her original *Tomb Raider* adventure – but a dinosaur? And not a run-of-the-mill dinosaur, either, but a ferocious *Tyrannosaurus rex*! Needless to say, discretion proved to be the better part of valour – which is to say that the best way to survive this prehistoric close encounter was to run as quickly as possible!

She's got it licked

Lara Croft was the **first female videogame protagonist on a postage stamp**. She was joined by Super Mario and the Prince of Persia among others when the *Héros des Jeux Vidéo* (Videogame Heroes) stamp collection was made available in France in 2005.

Big hit for a small team

UK-based Core Design had a team of just six – including Lara Croft's creator, Toby Gard (inset) – working on the original *Tomb Raider* from 1993 to 1996.

First female game protagonist to record an album

Lara faces the music in her games – but apparently she can make it, too. Musician Dave Stewart worked with model Rhona Mitra to create songs as though composed by the heroine herself. *Female Icon* (1999, above) was a France-only limited release.

EVOLUTION

Alongside Super Mario, Lara helped pioneer 3D gaming as we know it. And thankfully her appearance has become less jagged over the years…

Tomb Raider (1996)

Tomb Raider II (1997)

Tomb Raider III (1998)

The Angel of Darkness (2003)

Underworld (2008)

Tomb Raider (2013)

Shadow of the Tomb Raider (2018)

MOST UBIQUITOUS PLAYABLE FEMALE GAME CHARACTER

Some of Lara Croft's most iconic games are pictured in our Evolution panel (left). Gather these and all her other adventures together and she has starred in 23 titles across all formats since her 1996 debut. This puts clear daylight between Lara and those who would aim to take her crown as gaming's number-one female action icon. Expect more from Lara in the near future, too, with further adventures in Square Enix's successful *Tomb Raider* reboot set to follow in the wake of 2018's *Shadow of the Tomb Raider*.

8.5 MILLION

Crystal Dynamics' acclaimed reboot of the franchise in 2013 has resulted in the **best-selling *Tomb Raider* game**. Publisher Square Enix reported that *Tomb Raider* had flown off the shelves, selling a million copies in its opening two days on sale. It continued to sell well, shifting as many as 8.5 million copies by Apr 2015 – 1.5 million more than the original *Tomb Raider* (1996).

ARTHUR MORGAN

He may be an outlaw of the Wild West, but Arthur Morgan is still a hero at heart. The gunslinger blazes a trail through the worst, most lawless bandits that Rockstar's *Red Dead Redemption 2* (*RDR2*) can throw at him.

WANTED
DEAD OR ALIVE

REWARD: $1,500

First to achieve the maximum bounty level in *Red Dead Redemption 2*

A life of crime comes with its own risks. Unlawful activity in *RDR2* unleashes the full force of the law on Arthur, as well as a posse of bounty hunters. On 29 Oct 2018, just three days after the game's release, "Dat Saintsfan" uploaded a YouTube video in which he fought off the Pinkertons for long enough to put a $1,500 bounty on his head.

1,200 ACTORS

A huge 1,200 actors contributed their performances to *RDR2* – the **largest cast for a videogame**. Roger Clark provided the gravelly tones of Arthur Morgan and Benjamin Byron Davis voiced Dutch van der Linde.

Quickest on the draw

On 15 Dec 2017, Rockstar announced that those who unlocked the Double-Action Revolver in *GTA Online* (2013) would also own the weapon in *RDR2*. This made it the **first unlockable *GTA Online* weapon available in *RDR2***.

DOUBLE-ACTION REVOLVER

WEAPON SELECT

Having the right tools for the job is important in any line of work. It just so happens that the tools of an outlaw's trade are pistols, shotguns and rifles. Here, we reveal the most expensive arsenal that Arthur can assemble. That is, if your wallet is up to it.

Repeating Shotgun

$185

Rolling Block Rifle

$187

NEMESIS

As the head of the Van der Linde Gang, Dutch van der Linde is Arthur Morgan's boss. At first, the two see eye to eye, but the savageness of the Wild West starts to take its toll on Dutch, and he begins to abandon any trace of morality.

$1,250

The **most expensive horse in *RDR2*** is the Rose Grey Bay Arabian. The fast and hardy steed costs $1,250 and must be purchased from Blackwater Stable. As well as the high cost of the horse, Blackwater Stable becomes accessible only towards the end of the game.

A DYNAMITE YEAR...

As the saloon doors closed on 2018, *RDR2* rode into the sunset as the year's **best-selling game**, despite the title not being released until 26 Oct 2018. Rockstar's western sold a combined 13,940,203 physical units across the PS4 and Xbox One, as verified by VGChartz. The game's average review score, 96.45% as of 6 Mar 2019, verified by GameRankings, made it the year's **most critically acclaimed videogame**, too.

Carcano Rifle	Semi-Automatic Pistol	Semi-Auto Shotgun	Mauser Pistol
$190	$210	$225	$250

Largest development team for a videogame

According to *RDR2*'s producer Rob Nelson, roughly 2,000 Rockstar employees worked on bringing Arthur Morgan's adventures to life. Of these, 1,600 were engaged directly in the game's development. This dwarfs the estimated 1,000-strong development team on Rockstar's previous monster hit, *GTA V* (2013).

LOVE STORY

There was a time when Mary Gillis and Arthur were very much in love. That was before he became an outlaw and a member of the Van der Linde Gang. During *RDR2*, a family crisis forces Mary to get in touch with her first love, but their relationship seems destined to be one of missed opportunities.

85

LET'S GET READY TO RUMBLE

Shao Kahn

The Outworld realm's supreme ruler keeps on coming back for more. First appearing in Midway's *Mortal Kombat II* (1993), Shao Kahn has featured in a total of five titles – the **most boss appearances in *Mortal Kombat* games**. He beats fellow *Mortal Kombat* evil-doer Shinnok, who has awaited players in three of the series' titles.

Name: Shao Kahn
Game: Mortal Kombat 11 (Warner Bros., 2019)
Signature move: Emperor's Bash
Catchphrase: "You weak, pathetic fool!"

Harley Quinn

The gleefully anarchic DC super-villain is the **most recently created female character in *Injustice 2*.** Harley made her first appearance in an episode of *Batman: The Animated Series* on 11 Sep 1992. She appeared in *Injustice 2* 24 years 242 days later.

Name: Harley Quinn
Game: *Injustice 2* (Warner Bros, 2017)
Signature move: Hungry Hyenas
Catchphrase: "Prepare to be perforated!"

Wolverine

"Jwong" (aka Justin Wong, USA) – winner of the **most Evolution Championship Series titles** – often plays with the adamantium-clawed mutant on his team. Eight of his nine titles were won while playing games in Capcom's *Marvel vs. Capcom* fighting-game franchise.

Name: Wolverine
Game: Ultimate Marvel vs. Capcom 3 (Capcom, 2011)
Signature move: Weapon X
Catchphrase: "My claws have been aching for some action!"

Link

Legend of Zelda icon Link is the **first videogame guest character to appear in a *SoulCalibur* title**. The Hyrulian appeared in the GameCube version of *SoulCalibur II* in 2003. He shares the record with Heihachi Mishima – a veteran of *Tekken* (Bandai Namco, 1994) – who also appeared in *SoulCalibur II* on the PS2.

Name: Link
Game: SoulCalibur II (Bandai Namco, 2003)
Signature move: Cyclone Attack
Catchphrase: "Haaah-yah!"

Lili

Introduced in *Tekken 5: Dark Resurrection* (2006), Emilie de Rochefort – Lili for short – was used in the grand finals of the Tokyo Tekken Masters 2018 by "Knee" (aka Bae Jae-min, KOR). The **highest-ranked *Tekken 7* player** had claimed 286,850 ranking points, across 32 events, as of 13 Mar 2019.

Name: Lili

Game: *Tekken 7* (Bandai Namco, 2017)

Signature move: Matterhorn

Catchphrase: "You surely don't believe you can beat me?"

Name: Zamasu (Fused)

Game: *Dragon Ball FighterZ* (Bandai Namco, 2018)

Signature move: Eternal Justice

Catchphrase: "I am the wisdom, the law and the power of the universe!"

We've selected a knockout compilation of the fiercest fighters to ever punch, kick and throw their way through the most hotly contested fighting games on the pro tour. Only the top players can master each character's signature special moves, counters and ultimate combos.

Zamasu (Fused)

Dragon Ball FighterZ character Zamasu (Fused) was a go-to for "SonicFox" (aka Dominique McLean) as the fighting-game pro won the EVO 2018 Grand Finals. As of 18 Mar 2019, the American had earned the **most prize money by a fighting-game player** – $526,390 (£395,801) from 75 tournaments.

Akuma

The demonic Akuma had a big hand in "Tokido" (aka Hajime Taniguchi) becoming the **highest-ranked *Street Fighter V* player ever**. As of 13 Mar 2019, the pro gamer, who largely plays as Akuma, had a lifetime tournament score of 305,338, according to the tracking site Shoryuken.

Name: Akuma

Game: *Street Fighter V* (Capcom, 2016)

Signature move: Raging Demon

Catchphrase: "You will feel my wrath!"

Name: Jigglypuff

Game: *Super Smash Bros. Ultimate* (Nintendo, 2018)

Signature move: Puff Up

Catchphrase: "Jiggly!"

Jigglypuff

The highest-earning *Super Smash Bros.* player is "Hungrybox" (aka Juan DeBiedma, USA), who's known for using the often-overlooked Jigglypuff in tournaments. As of 13 Mar 2019, "Hungrybox" had won $320,149 (£243,590) from the 265 events he'd competed in.

MAKE YOUR OWN CHARACTER

Not all games have a specific character at their heart. In fact, some would rather make *you* their hero. Such games offer you the chance to create your own avatar before the adventure begins...

Most used Javelin exosuit in *Anthem*

In EA's *Anthem* (2019), players have the chance to choose what their human counterpart looks like in the game. But more importantly, they can also choose the type of flying exosuit, known in the game as a Javelin, that they'll wear for heading into battle. According to official figures provided to us by EA on 3 Apr 2019, the most used Javelin was the Storm, with 28.5% of players wearing the suit during expeditions. By comparison, 25.3% used the Ranger, 23.7% the Colossus and 22.5% the Interceptor.

COMING UP ▶▶▶▶

PUBG

PLAYERUNKNOWN'S BATTLEGROUNDS (we'll stick to *PUBG*) has held its own as the battle royale of choice for many gamers. Like other titles in the genre, all you have to do to win is survive… but that's easier said than done when you're in a war zone.

Highest-earning team

If you bump into any members of OMG while playing *PUBG*, we advise you to run for cover and stay there. As of 5 Mar 2019, the Chinese team had won $724,643 (£548,555) across 16 pro tournaments.

OMG's preferred first team when it comes to *PUBG* events includes the players "lionkk" (aka Yao Hao), "silentBT_" (Wang Yan) and "xiaohaixxxx" (Zhang Jinhai). But if one of those is unavailable, they have a host of other (just as deadly) replacements waiting in reserve. You should pay particular attention to "lionkk", whose statistics speak for themselves (see below).

TOOLS OF THE TRADE

Like the world's most diverse fancy dress contest, *PUBG* lets players deck themselves out in a huge variety of outfits and accessories. Who knows, perhaps the Epic-grade clothing we've selected will dazzle your opponents and give you an edge.

Horse Mask — Stay hip to the trot with this festive mask

Medieval Helmet — Look like a knight of old with this helmet

Ancient Mummy Mask — Scare your opponents into submission

Most viewed fan film

In "*PUBG*: Ek Game Katha", real people are dropped inside the *PUBG* world. As of 11 Mar 2019, the comedy video had been viewed 34,091,284 times! It was published on YouTube on 21 Nov 2018 by its producer, Ashish Chanchlani (IND).

Highest-earning player

As of 12 Feb 2019, Chinese gamer "lionkk" (aka Yao Hao) had earned $198,927 (£154,221) from 16 *PUBG* tournaments. His haul includes a $107,500 (£81,997) share from winning the *PUBG* Global Invitational on 29 Jul 2018 alongside his team, OMG (see above). "As a professional, I play games to win," he said.

LONGEST TIME FOR A GAME TO MAINTAIN 1 MILLION DAILY PLAYERS ON STEAM

For 366 days, between 8 Sep 2017 and 9 Sep 2018, *PUBG* (2017) maintained 1 million daily players on Steam, a feat demonstrating the enduring popularity of PUBG Corporation's battle royale. According to SteamDB, the game's daily player count finally dipped below the million mark – to 960,263 – on 10 Sep 2018.

Sunglasses
Look cool, even if your pulse is racing.

Hoodie
Luxury leathers are the height of *PUBG* fashion.

Work Pants
Live dangerously in these bright trousers.

Parachute
Arrive on the battlefield in style.

Most players banned from a game (overall)

Unofficial third-party hacks can be used to locate players on *PUBG* maps. As this is critical to victory, it was soon outlawed. According to the Official Korean *PUBG* Cafe website, more than 13 million accounts were banned from Jun 2017 to Oct 2018. Then another 30,000 players were kicked out in Dec 2018!

Most solo top 10 finishes

According to PUBGTracker, expert survivor "didwjd" had held on to a place in the final 10 players in 888 of the 1,269 rounds they'd taken part in, as of 15 Feb 2019. This was 191 more top 10 placements than the 697 recorded by the nearest rival, "DouYu-2210156".

91

WORLD OF WARCRAFT

Blizzard's MMORPG is one of the all-time gaming greats. The expansions to the 2004 original have made sure that *WoW* continues to inspire gamers to create a character, choose a side and give their all for the cause.

WoW's most expensive mount

The "Reins of the Mighty Caravan Brutosaur" is a dinosaur-like beast that was added to *WoW* on 14 Aug 2018 as part of the *Battle for Azeroth* expansion. The mount carries an auction house on its back, so that whoever owns it can buy and sell goods anywhere. It's a great help if you can afford one, but at the eye-watering price of 5 million units of in-game gold, few will be able to. Mind you, they do say you have to spend money to make it...

$598,999

As of 25 Sep 2018, a total of 8,379 backers raised $598,999 (£456,825) to make *The WoW Diary* the **most funded non-fiction book project on Kickstarter**. The book is by John Staats, *WoW*'s first 3D-level designer, who began documenting the game's development in 2001. He called it "a rare, unfiltered, comprehensive look at game development".

TOOLS OF THE TRADE

Any *WoW* adventurer should make sure they have all of the equipment they need to stay alive in its hostile world. This is especially true in the game's climactic raids, where you'll need every bit of help you can lay your hands on in order to emerge victorious.

Flasks
Store your potions and medicines

Food
Restores health and grants boosts

First player to reach *WoW: Battle for Azeroth* level cap

Denmark's "Gingi" (aka Mike Djebbara) invited the world to watch him reach *Battle for Azeroth*'s level cap (set at level 120) live on Twitch. The Method guild member managed it just five hours after the expansion launched on 14 Aug 2018.

First player to collect every achievement in *WoW: Legion*

On 22 Mar 2018, "Xirev" (SWE) earned all 3,314 achievements in *WoW: Legion*. Completing all achievements means (among other things) reaching Prestige 25, winning 5,000 pet battles against other players and finishing the "Antorus, the Burning Throne" raid on Mythic difficulty.

FIRST GUILD TO BEAT G'HUUN RAID IN *BATTLE FOR AZEROTH* (MYTHIC)

On 19 Sep 2018, the famous *WoW* guild Method streamed its successful attempt to defeat the Blood God G'huun (below) on Twitch. The run involved tackling the *Battle for Azeroth*'s first raid on Mythic difficulty – the most challenging mode there is.

The "G'huun Uldir" raid was added to *WoW* on 4 Sep 2018, but the Mythic difficulty wasn't unlocked until 11 Sep, prompting a keenly contested race to be the first guild to defeat it.

WORLD OF WARCRAFT
BATTLE FOR AZEROTH

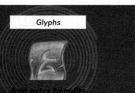

Enchants	Glyphs	Containers	Spell Books
Infuse equipment with magical effects.	Add extra benefits to your spells.	All the space you need for your loot.	Record your spells for future use.

First Stan Lee cameo in an MMO

In Jan 2019, Blizzard honoured late Marvel legend Stan Lee by adding a non-player character (NPC) with his likeness to *WoW*. Known as "Stanley" and bearing Lee's unmistakable moustache, he can be found in Stormwind City. He even says Lee's signature catchphrase "Excelsior!" to passers-by.

Rarest *WoW* trading card

The "Spectral Tiger" Ally card is the most elusive in the *World of Warcraft Trading Card Game*. It was issued as part of the "Fires of Outland" expansion, but it appeared in only one out of every 484 booster packs. *WoW* trading cards are no longer being printed, but in Mar 2019 a "Spectral Tiger" example with an unscratched code (meaning it might still be redeemed online for use in the game) was found. It was listed on eBay for $2,750 (£2,108)!

93

DESTINY 2

Following the original *Destiny* was always going to be a challenge – and so it proved when Activision's *Destiny 2* received a mixed reaction from fans. However, skip forward a few months and the game's "Forsaken" DLC has restored the series' reputation.

Best PvP Guardian K/D ratio

When honing their skills against other players in the Crucible, Guardians can set themselves apart with an impressive Kill/Death (K/D) ratio. As of 28 Feb 2019, PS4 player "L-Divine-Zero-L" had the best ratio at 41:1 (meaning the player has 41 kills for each death suffered). The impressive stats were verified by DestinyTracker.

Most pledges received for a faction rally

Destiny 2's seasonal Faction Rallies are hives of activity in which Guardians undertake missions to support a preferred vendor. Pledges across the three factions during Season 3 totalled close to 5 million. Of these, 2,019,311 pledges went to Dead Orbit (above left), putting the sombre Faction ahead of New Monarchy (1,560,283) and Future War Cult (1,218,803).

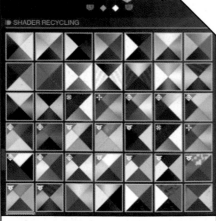

Most unwanted reward item

If gamers hate one thing, it's being laden with needless baggage. When *Destiny 2* introduced Shaders, which change the colour and sheen of armour and weapons, exasperated gamers soon ended up with hundreds of them. This led to 807,635,124 Shader deletions inside 77 days, according to series developer Bungie. "A time-consuming mess," said one player.

Rarest weapon

The Redrix's Claymore pulse rifle is the most difficult weapon to obtain in *Destiny 2*. In an infographic released on 2 Aug 2018, Bungie revealed that only 8,750 players owned the gun. To get their hands on it, players had to first purchase the "Warmind" DLC, then win hundreds of Glory Crucible matches to hit the required "Fabled" rank.

TOOLS OF THE TRADE

Even Guardians need a little bit of help to fight back against Dominus Ghaul and his army. Here, we take a look at the items that should be on your radar.

Ghost
Get back on your feet with the help of these sentient machines.

Sparrow
Save your tired legs by sitting astride one of these hoverbikes.

Ship
Take the controls to start planet-hopping across the Milky Way.

Region Chests
Keep 'em peeled for these loot-filled treasure chests.

Dusklight Shard
Infuse those Exotic weapons with this valuable resource.

FASTEST COMPLETION OF THE "LAST WISH" RAID

Expectation was high for *Destiny 2*'s "Forsaken" expansion, released in Sep 2018. Focus immediately fell on to the DLC's "Last Wish" raid, the latest in *Destiny 2*'s notoriously tough challenges for teams of up to six players. On 26 Nov 2018, in a display of coordination and dedication, Wrath – a clan made up of members "Jazzwastaken" (COL), "DarkXBL", "REEclipse" (CAN), "ItsScrub", "Zinsa" (both USA) and "Stamina" – took 20 min 58 sec to blast through to the raid's conclusion, as verified by Speedrun.

Most-followed *Destiny 2* streamer on Twitch

As well as being a renowned *Destiny 2* player, American "KingGothalion" is a popular Twitch broadcaster. The streamer, known for his love of "looter shooters", had attracted 919,656 followers to his Twitch channel as of 28 Feb 2019, a figure verified by SocialBlade.

95

SEA OF THIEVES

If you like to sing "Yo ho, yo ho! A pirate's life for me" at the top of your lungs while hoisting the Jolly Roger, then *Sea of Thieves* is the game for you. Rare's piratical MMORPG lets gamers sail the high seas, loot booty and even walk the plank...

Fastest time to raid a Skeleton Fort

When players spy an ominous skull-shaped green cloud glowering in the sky, it indicates that a Skeleton Fort has materialized. To protect their evil Skeleton Captain within, the undead patrol the fort and fire cannons at passing ships.

Fort raids often take an hour or more to defeat, but it took YouTuber "Gladd" and his first mate "Modern Tryhard" just 10 min to topple one such stronghold, in a YouTube video posted on 27 Mar 2018.

First "Pirate Legend" in *Sea of Thieves*

Twitch streamer "Prod1gyx" raced to become the first player to gain Pirate Legend status. He hit the necessary level 50 across the game's three trading companies – Gold Hoarders, Order of Souls and Merchant Alliance – on 29 Mar 2018, just nine days after the title's release date.

First game to allow players to collaboratively run a ship

Released on 20 Mar 2018, *Sea of Thieves* is the first game to allow players to crew a ship, with up to four players able to set sail together. It also offers gaming's **first shared-world pirating adventure**, where your motley crew can fight (or befriend) other pirate ships manned by rival sets of players.

Farthest human-cannonball flight

To start *Sea of Thieves'* launch with a bang, Microsoft arranged for human cannonball "The Bullet" (aka David Smith Jr, USA) to challenge his existing record. In Florida, USA, on 13 Mar 2018, he flew 59.43 m (195 ft) – 0.38 m (1 ft 2 in) farther than ever before.

To become a mighty pirate (and not the Guybrush Threepwood kind), players must learn to make use of more than just their good looks and quick wits...

Spyglass

Get a closer look at whatever *that* is on the horizon.

Compass

Use it to count your paces when looking for buried treasure.

Cannonball

Your best attack and defence, so stow plenty on your ship!

Lantern

A handy light and a vital weapon against shadow skeletons.

Tankard

Pirates have to party – just don't overdo the grog!

FASTEST-SELLING NEW XBOX ONE IP

Shortly after *Sea of Thieves* set sail on 20 Mar 2018, Microsoft declared Rare's game to be the fastest-selling new Microsoft-owned intellectual property (IP) of its generation. As verified by VGChartz, more than a million players were active upon launch day, climbing to over two million in the game's first week of sale. "We've been blown away by how the game has brought players together," read a post on the official Xbox website.

Most-viewed megalodon encounter

On 29 May 2018, Microsoft launched the "Hungering Deep" DLC, in which the monstrous megalodon made its debut. The encounter between YouTuber "jackfrags" (UK) and the prehistoric shark had amassed 4,225,980 views as of 11 Jan 2019.

FALLOUT

Who thought that surviving a nuclear blast would be the easy bit? If Bethesda's *Fallout* series is any guide to the apocalypse, wandering the wastelands will be fraught with even more danger – be that from mutants, beasts or mutant beasts...

First online multiplayer *Fallout* game

Fallout Tactics: Brotherhood of Steel (2001) let players form squads of wastelanders and compete online in turn-based combat. This made it the first *Fallout* game you could play online – and it proved far less divisive with the series' loyal fanbase than the similarly online *Fallout 76* (2018).

Fastest completion of all five *Fallout* main-series games

On 21 Jul 2018, speed-runner "tomatoanus" (USA) cleared *Fallout*'s five single-player entries (comprising *Fallout 1–4* and 2010's *New Vegas*) in just 1 hr 29 min 47 sec, as verified by Speedrun. The gamer used glitches and his own experience to find the shortest routes.

TOOLS OF THE TRADE

The wastelands of *Fallout* are not to be ventured into without being fully prepared for whatever lies in wait. Guns and other weapons are a must, but certain other items are just as vital if you're going to survive while exploring the game's hostile world.

Pip-Boy — Everything an explorer needs, all on the wrist.

Power Armour — The last word in battle-ready tech.

Nuka-Cola — A fizzy treat in an uncivilized world.

48 MIN 25 SEC

On 28 Apr 2018, "BubblesDelFuego" (aka Tucker Olinsky, USA) ran through *Fallout 4 VR* (2017) to set a new best time for the game's "Real Time Attack" run (meaning his time was against the clock with no breaks). He exploited the game's teleportation controls to cover ground quickly.

50.84%

Since its release in Nov 2018, *Fallout 76* has staggered through a critical wasteland. As of 4 Mar 2019, the PS4 version is the **lowest-ranked western-style RPG** on GameRankings, with an average score of 50.84% across its 25 reviews. One critic called the online title "of little consequence" as well as "big, ugly and unloved".

FIRST NUKE DROP IN *FALLOUT 76*

It didn't take long for the first mushroom cloud to rise up in *Fallout 76*. On 14 Nov 2018, the day of the game's release, the "Appalachian Explorers" team ("Nickaroo93", "Pure_Savagery", "Polaflex", "Ancker", "Augura" and "Sam00197") became the first wastelanders to locate the nuclear silo, find the launch codes and trigger the game's "Scorched Earth" finale.

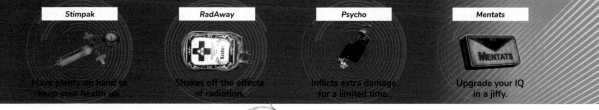

Stimpak	RadAway	Psycho	Mentats
Have plenty on hand to keep your health up.	Shakes off the effects of radiation.	Inflicts extra damage for a limited time.	Upgrade your IQ in a jiffy.

Most signatures for a *Fallout 76* petition

Fallout fans famously value the series' single-player gameplay. So much so that, in protest over *Fallout 76*'s move to an online experience, thousands made their feelings clear through a change.org petition. As of 4 Mar 2019, 20,857 gamers had signed the "Keep the Lone Wanderer Wandering Alone" appeal.

First player to fly in *Fallout 76*

It took some weird science for YouTuber "TYR" to achieve flight – or the closest thing to it – in *Fallout 76*. "TYR" combined the game's "Marsupial" and "Bird Bones" mutations with a special perk and the help of a few friends to enable him to fly like Superman above the game's scorched landscapes.

MINECRAFT

Creating your own character is one thing; creating a whole universe to go with it is another – but that's the genius of *Minecraft*. For a decade, it has been inspiring a generation of gamers to indulge their imaginations one block at a time.

Largest live music concert in *Minecraft*
On 12–13 Jan 2019, the Fire Festival was viewed by 87,754 fans. Of those, 5,300 players attended by loading their avatar on to the event's server, while everyone else watched via streams on the festival's website and on its Discord channel. Headliners included Hudson Mohawke and Slumberjack.

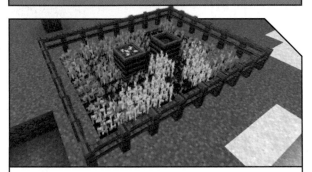

First composting mechanic
Recycling is just as important in a virtual world as it is in the real world. That's why *Minecraft*'s developer Mojang added a composter to its game in 2019. The device lets players turn plants and other organic material into bone meal, which can then be used to speed up the growth of new plants.

74,129 DOWNLOADS
Avatar skins can be based on just about anything – even videogame characters. The **most popular game-inspired *Minecraft* skin** is that of *The Legend of Zelda*'s Link, designed by "Zach8460" in 2011. As of 7 Mar 2019, it had been downloaded from the Planet Minecraft website 74,129 times. Its closest rival was a skin based on Altaïr from *Assassin's Creed*, with 66,276 downloads.

Get miaow of here!
In Oct 2018, Mojang ran a poll to add one of its players' cats to the game. After what it called a "fierce feline competition", Jellie – owned by "GoodTimesWithScar" (aka Ryan Anderson) – became the **first real-life pet officially added to *Minecraft***. As a result, there are now 11 cat avatars in *Minecraft*.

TOOLS OF THE TRADE
Whatever your ambitions when it comes to building and crafting, there are a few trusted tools that you'll always want close to hand. Here, we list *Minecraft*'s essential items.

Sword
Don't face any mobs without this...

Bow
Takes care of enemies at distance.

Pickaxe
Mines for valuables or smashes objects apart.

Shovel
Digs through soil and sand faster.

Fishing Rod
Who knows what you'll catch...

FIRST INTERACTIVE TV SHOW BASED ON A VIDEOGAME

Minecraft: Story Mode (2015) was one of developer Telltale Games' final acts (see pp.8–9). The multiple-choice adventure game was even adapted for Netflix. In Nov 2018, an interactive show was launched for the TV-streaming platform. Just as with the game, it let viewers choose how the story of Jesse (right), Olivia and Axel played out.

Reader challenges

In last year's *Gamer's Edition*, we invited you to step forward and attempt to become a world-beater, just like "SeaPeeKay" (aka Callum Knight, UK, left). See the table on the right to find out who proved themselves to be a *Minecraft* master. Then turn to pp.62–63 to read about this year's *Fortnite* challenges.

RECORD	NAME	TIME
Fastest time to build a castle in Creative mode (PC)	Parham Galahroudi (DEU)	3:22.23
Fastest time to build a castle in Creative mode (console)	Tristen Geren (USA)	5:01
Fastest time to saddle/stable 10 horses in Survival mode	Šimon Chlouba (CZE)	3:45.01

NEW HERO

This year's book is bursting with famous heroes, but what of those champions whose adventures are just beginning? Here, we take a look at the next generation of gaming icons who are out to fight the good fight...

WOLF

The star of *Sekiro: Shadows Die Twice* (Activision, 2019) is a ninja with a mechanical arm – it's no wonder gamers like him! Deflecting attacks is the key to defeating Wolf's many enemies. As of 3 Apr 2019, "Darnildo" (CAN) had done just that to topple 45,345 hostiles – the **most enemies defeated** – on the Xbox One version, as verified by TrueAchievements.

THE PRISONER

In Motion Twin's *Dead Cells* (2018), gamers play as an unnamed hero – often referred to as "The Prisoner" by fans. The roguelike platformer has gone down a storm with speed-runners. The USA's "Rockstomb" achieved the **fastest completion of *Dead Cells: The Hand of the King*** in 7 min 33 sec, as verified by Speedrun on 5 May 2019.

SOPHIA & JESSICA BLAZKOWICZ

Wolfenstein: Youngblood (2019) took the series in a new direction by forcing its usual lead B J Blazkowicz into the background and installing his twin daughters into the driving seat. As a result, Bethesda's shooter is the **first FPS with twins as its leads**. We first met Jess (far left) and Soph in a dream sequence in *Wolfenstein: The New Order* (2014) – now here they are causing a nightmare for *Youngblood*'s villains.

ZORA & RASHIDA

In the Valley of Gods sees an intrepid duo (Zora is pictured right) bidding to restore their reputations as explorers seeking hidden treasures in Egypt. Aptly, the pair are also about to restore Valve's reputation as a publisher of videogames. When it's released in (we think) late 2019, the game will mark the **longest time between single-player Valve games**, with around eight years passing since the release of *Portal 2* in 2011!

AUDITIONS

GUINNESS WORLD RECORDS

THE KNIGHT

In the miniature world of *Hollow Knight* (Team Cherry, 2017), the Knight is on a quest to find the source of a deadly infection that's killing the kingdom's residents. The toughest speed-run involves unlocking the game's "True Ending" – something that's possible only if you know all of its secrets. According to Speedrun, the **fastest "True Ending" completion** is by "vysuals" (USA) in 1 hr 7 min 28 sec, as verified on 5 Mar 2019.

MADELINE

Super-hard but totally charming, *Celeste* made gamers fall in love with the 2D platformer genre all over again when it was released in Jan 2018. At the heart of the love story is Madeline, the game's courageous main character. As of 13 Mar 2018, the platformer from Matt Makes Games is **the highest-rated indie game on Xbox One** according to GameRankings, where it has an aggregated score of 96%.

ZAGREUS

Epic might make the most headlines with *Fortnite*, but the publisher also launched an online game store to rival Steam in 2019. The Epic Store is already securing exclusive games, with Supergiant Games' *Hades* the store's **first exclusive third-party game.** In the roguelike dungeon crawler, Zagreus will fight his way through the Greek underworld to defy the god of death.

V

It's not even out and already CD Projekt Red's *Cyberpunk 2077* is setting records. Its reveal trailer was the **most-watched trailer for a new IP debuted at E3 2018**. As of 2 Apr 2019, it had been viewed 17,160,767 times since being added to YouTube on 10 Jun 2018. Once it arrives, expect to play as V – an up-and-coming cyberpunk in a dystopian future.

SURVIVORS

Facing off against invading aliens, zombie hordes and terrifying demons is a daily job for these heroes. You can be sure that when the battle's over and the smoke has cleared, they'll be the ones left standing.

Most consecutive wins in *Honor of Kings*

With 332 consecutive wins in Tencent's 2015 MOBA *Honor of Kings* (called *Arena of Valor* in the west), all eyes were on Chinese e-sports pro "Saobai" as he went for win number 333 on 26 Jan 2019. The match – played in Beijing, China – was streamed live on Twitch, with 15 million people tuning in. Despite all the added pressure of the occasion, nerves didn't get the better of "Saobai". The gamer, well known for wearing his silver mask, marched to his 333rd victory. The number 333 is regarded as lucky in Chinese culture.

GUINNESS WORLD RECORDS

CERTIFICATE

The most consecutive wins in
Honor of Kings
is 333 and was achieved by
Saobai (China)
in Beijing, China,
on 26 January 2019

OFFICIALLY AMAZING

RECORD HOLDER

COMING UP ▶▶▶

APEX LEGENDS

Apex Legends took the battle-royale scene by storm when EA stealth-launched the title in early 2019. Gamers have downloaded the free-to-play FPS in droves, with each player setting their sights on being the champion.

1,001 FULL SQUAD WINS

Winning a round without losing a squad member takes some doing. As of 3 Apr 2019, "xshoT" had achieved the **most full squad wins** with 1,001, as verified by ApexTracker. The feat meant that "xshoT" kept a vow made on Twitter, promising to hit 1,000 by 1 Apr 2019.

LEVEL 849

When *Apex* first launched, the unlockables earned for levelling-up ended at level 100. But that didn't stop "Joker47jk" (USA) from soldiering on... and on... and on. The persistent gamer is *Apex Legends*' **highest-level player**, hitting level 849 as of 23 Apr 2019. Going by his current rate, that figure will be way, way higher by the time you read this.

SNAPSHOT 📷

The search for the Loch Ness Monster has been going on for a long time, but it took gamers just eight days to track the creature down in *Apex Legends*. Players noticed 10 Loch Ness plushies in different locations. A period of trial and error followed before players found the right order in which to shoot them, resulting in "Nessie" rearing up in the misty swamplands.

WEAPON SELECT

When you're fighting for survival in *Apex Legends*, getting your hands on one of the best weapons could represent the difference between life and death. Here is a fearsome selection of the most devastating armaments in the game.

Mastiff	Peacekeeper	Spitfire
Wastes anyone who strays too close.	More death-dealer than peacekeeper, in truth.	Combines accuracy with a threat of damage.

Most kills

Accuracy is pretty much everything in EA's battle royale. Of all the players, it's "basedgodfearless" (aka James Fearless) who has been the best at making his shots count. As of 3 Apr 2019, the American PC player had taken out 23,721 opponents. A huge majority of those eliminations – 22,696 in total – had been carried out in the guise of the dimensional rift-hopping fighter Wraith.

Most revives

Apex Legends isn't all about the fighting... As of 3 Apr 2019, "MmmQyf" had revived 3,000 fellow players. The revival system allows a player to either help their comrade up when they've fallen or grab their banner from their body and take it to a Respawn Beacon. These are often situated in dangerous, exposed areas.

MOST REGISTERED PLAYERS FOR A FREE-TO-PLAY HERO-SHOOTER

The arrival of *Apex Legends* on 4 Feb 2019 was notable for the silence that preceded it. There was no year-long cycle of hype or fanfare. Instead, the game was suddenly just there. The lack of promotion created even more of a stir, helping *Apex* become an instant sensation. In a tweet on the official @PlayApex Twitter account, EA confirmed that the hero-shooter had amassed 50 million registered players as of 4 Mar 2019 – just one month after the title's launch.

Wingman	Kraber	Longbow	Devotion
Knocks down opponents with a few shots.	Slow-firing but particularly deadly.	Packs a punch over huge distances.	Eats ammo, but also cuts down enemies.

First DLC weapon

On 20 Feb 2019, EA released a trailer showcasing the Havoc rifle – the first new gun to be added to *Apex Legends*. It went live later the same day. The gun can fit two enhancing "hop-up" attachments. "Select Fire" gives you a powerful single-shot option, while "Turbocharger" speeds up the charging time of the rifle's beam blast.

Popular and not so...

With her healing drone and speedy teammate revival, Lifeline is the **most popular** *Apex Legends* **character**. As of 3 Apr 2019, the combat medic had been selected 18.6% of the time. That figure drops to 3.9% for Caustic – the **least popular character**. It doesn't help that his Nox Gas hampers squadmates.

107

DOOM SLAYER

DOOM's famous green marine has been a staple of gaming for over 26 years, but in all that time he's never had a settled name (see Quick Fact bar). Unlike his name, though, his capacity for taking on Hell's legions has never been in doubt.

Longest-running developer of FPS games

As of 21 Mar 2019, id Software (USA) had been developing shooters for 24 years 8 days. Its first FPS was *Wolfenstein 3D*, released on 5 May 1992, and its most recent was *DOOM* on 13 May 2016. The release of *DOOM Eternal* will extend it again.

Most ported FPS

Since it was released in 1993, *DOOM* has been ported to 20 different gaming platforms. And that's just the official count. There have also been dozens of unofficial ports to all kinds of computer devices, including calculators, digital cameras, in-car entertainment systems, smart fridges and even ATMs!

Most-travelled megawad?

A megawad is the old term for a pack of maps and extra content for *DOOM* (similar to a DLC pack). John Romero, one of *DOOM*'s original developers, is working on a new megawad called *SIGIL*. He's laboured in 11 countries and even while at sea – meaning that, though impossible to verify, *SIGIL* surely has a claim to be the most-travelled *DOOM* megawad ever!

WEAPON SELECT

There's no point trying to reason with the demons in *DOOM*. The only language they understand is extreme violence – and plenty of it. Here's a reminder of the weaponry with which the DOOM Slayer first faced off against Hell's minions in the original game of 1993.

Chainsaw — Leaves your enemies in a bloody heap.

Pistol — Carries loads of ammo, but is low on damage.

Shotgun — Packs a punch if things get up close and personal.

NEMESIS

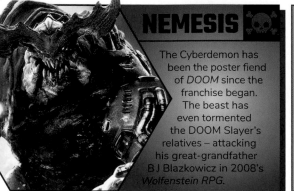

The Cyberdemon has been the poster fiend of *DOOM* since the franchise began. The beast has even tormented the DOOM Slayer's relatives – attacking his great-grandfather BJ Blazkowicz in 2008's *Wolfenstein RPG*.

21 MIN 0 SEC

On 24 Nov 2018, "KingDime" set the **fastest completion of episodes 1–4 on "Ultra Violence" difficulty** of ***Ultimate DOOM***, as verified by Speedrun. He braved the episodes "Knee-Deep in the Dead", "The Shores of Hell", "Inferno" and "Thy Flesh Consumed", but said it was failing to go under 21 min that would "haunt" him.

MOST APPEARANCES AS THE LEAD PROTAGONIST IN AN FPS

Over the past 26 years, the DOOM Slayer has provided plenty of evidence that he's even more unstoppable than the forces of Hell. The marine has taken the lead in 12 *DOOM* games, from id Software's 1993 original to Bethesda's *DOOM Eternal* (due in 2019). Over the years, the Slayer has only become stronger, with his recent appearances seeing him tearing through Hell's demons – often literally.

Chaingun	Rocket Launcher	Plasma Gun	BFG9000
Mows down enemies in a blur of bullets.	Makes even a Baron of Hell think twice.	Disintegrates demons without breaking sweat.	Unleashes destructive balls of deadly plasma.

NEXT APPEARANCE

DOOM Eternal is of particular interest to gamers, as it will be one of the titles that Google uses to promote its new videogame-streaming service Stadia (see pp.10–11). Let's hope that the technology allows the DOOM Slayer to save the world uninterrupted and free from connection troubles that could leave him holding his head in his hands.

Rarest achievement in *DOOM 3*

According to TrueAchievements, "Evil Nightmare" is the toughest achievement in *DOOM 3: BFG Edition* (2012) for the Xbox 360. It requires players to finish the "Resurrection of Evil" campaign on "Nightmare" difficulty. As of 27 Mar 2019, just 4% of players had completed the challenge.

109

SAMUS ARAN

Samus Aran has been travelling the galaxy for decades, but she doesn't call at Earth to drop off another of her missions as often as her fans might like. More's the pity, because whenever Samus's ship does come around, amazing adventures usually follow.

NEXT APPEARANCE

In early 2019, Nintendo announced that *Metroid Prime 4* was going back to the drawing board. Development of the game has returned to Retro Studios – who made the *Metroid Prime* trilogy – so at least there was some good news for fans.

First videogame protagonist to have a Faceship

Many egotistical villains have wanted a Faceship (a ship built in their own likeness) as a mode of travel, but it was Samus Aran who began the craze. Samus's gunship, made in the image of her helmet, was introduced in 1991's *Metroid II: Return of Samus* for the Game Boy.

40 MIN 56 SEC

The UK's "Behemoth87" and the US's "zoast" are battling over the **fastest completion of *Super Metroid***. On 6 Apr 2019, "Behemoth87" edged ahead with the fastest time yet, as verified by Speedrun.

NEMESIS ☠

Ridley is a dragon-turned-Space Pirate who is as cunning as he is ruthless. Samus has defeated him repeatedly, but he keeps coming back for more. This is largely because he can regenerate by consuming his enemies!

First videogame protagonist to use a freeze ray

Samus Aran brought her Ice Beam weapon to the gaming world in her 1986 debut. It allowed Samus to ice her foes so she could use them as platforms. It also just so happens that deep cold is the Metroids' weakness.

Longest time between *Metroid* releases

Metroid fans have become used to waiting for their next fix (see timeline below). *Super Metroid* (1994) is a timeless classic, but it didn't receive a sequel for 8 years 243 days. The drought was ended by *Metroid Prime* on 17 Nov 2002.

1.76 MILLION

The **best-selling handheld game with a playable female protagonist** is *Metroid II: Return of Samus* for the Game Boy. Nintendo's 2D side-scrolling adventure had sold 1.76 million physical copies as of 21 Mar 2019, as verified by VGChartz.

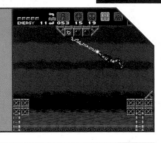

EVOLUTION
Whether seen in 2D side-scrollers, first-person shooters or third-person adventures, Samus has always been at the forefront of videogame visuals.

Metroid (1986, NES)

Metroid II: Return of Samus (1991, Game Boy)

Super Metroid (1994, Super Nintendo)

Metroid Prime (2002, GameCube)

Metroid Fusion (2002, GBA)

Metroid: Other M (2010, Wii)

Metroid: Samus Returns (2017, 3DS)

1986   1991   1994   2002   2002

MOST CRITICALLY ACCLAIMED FIRST-PERSON SHOOTER (FPS)

Taking *Metroid*'s iconic 2D-level design and moulding it into the 3D environments of a first-person shooter seemed like a gamble at the time. But when *Metroid Prime* was released in 2002, it proved to be an instant hit. As of 27 Mar 2019, the recognized classic had an average score of 96.33% across 87 reviews on GameRankings – higher than any other FPS, including *Halo: Combat Evolved* (Microsoft) and *Half-Life 2* (Valve).

2004

2004

2006

2007

2010

2017

LEON & CLAIRE

When Leon S Kennedy and Claire Redfield arrived in Raccoon City at the start of 1998's *Resident Evil 2* (Capcom), neither character expected to be battling zombies for 20 years and counting. Their pain is most definitely our gain.

First episodic *Resident Evil* game

Resident Evil: Revelations 2 (2015) came to PS4, Xbox One and other platforms in a series of four downloadable episodes. The first instalment was released on 24 Feb 2015, with subsequent episodes spaced one week apart, each with an appetite-whetting cliffhanger. The complete season was then released in both physical and digital formats on 18 Mar 2015, with additional content included.

Most kills in *Resident Evil 6*

To create a faster-paced experience, *Resident Evil 6* (2012) was more third-person shooter than survival horror. As of 15 Apr 2019, its deadliest player was "Joye", who had taken out 379,999,962 zombies (and worse) on the Xbox 360.

NEMESIS ☠

As far as the public are concerned, the Umbrella Corporation supplies vital drugs. Leon and Claire know better, though, discovering that the conglomerate's real goal is to make indestructible bio-weapons (including zombies).

WEAPON SELECT

For the 2019 version of *Resident Evil 2*, Capcom has revisited the weaponry from the original game, improving and adding to it to give Leon and Claire more of a fighting chance. It's a good job, too, because the zombies are harder to kill than ever. Here are just a few of the new and overhauled items that are at Leon and Claire's disposal.

Combat Knife

Stops a zombie from biting you.

Flash Grenade

Stuns enemies with sound and light.

80%

With four out of five choosing the rookie Raccoon City police officer, Leon is by far the **most popular first-playthrough character in *Resident Evil 2*.** As of 25 Mar 2019, Leon's journey had been attempted by more gamers overall too, with more than 7 million beginning his campaign versus the 5.1 million who'd played as Claire.

Most time-consuming puzzle in *Resident Evil 2*

Of all the brain teasers in 2019's *Resident Evil 2*, the "Plug Socket" puzzle has confounded the most gamers. As of 1 Apr 2019, players had spent the equivalent of 32,623 days deciphering it. The tricky puzzle requires gamers to arrange chess pieces in the correct order to open a door in the sewers.

Pawn Plug
Key item
A pawn-shaped electrical connector.

FASTEST COMPLETION OF
RESIDENT EVIL 2 (2019)

It turns out that Claire's campaign takes slightly less time to complete than Leon's in the 2019 remake. On 25 Mar 2019, "7rayD" (FIN) finished a "Standard" difficulty run as Claire in 50 min 38 sec, as verified by Speedrun. By contrast, the **fastest completion of Leon's campaign** was set by "Orchlon" (MNG), who took 53 min 2 sec on 4 Apr 2019. It's impressive just how closely matched Capcom was able to make its characters' main missions.

Hand Grenade	Spark Shot Stungun	Lightning Hawk Magnum	Minigun
Inflicts maximum damage from minimum effort.	Shocks your targets with a well-aimed zap.	Blasts huge holes in the zombie hordes.	Turns the undead into the very dead.

Rarest cause of death in *Resident Evil 2*

Of the many and varied grisly fates that can await Leon and Claire in 2019's *Resident Evil 2*, being blown up is the least likely. As of 25 Mar 2019, only 0.24% of deaths had been due to perishing in an explosion. That works out at just one in every 450 deaths. A much more likely demise is being "Smashed" (ouch!), which accounts for 9.53% of all deaths.

Most critically acclaimed survival-horror game

Resident Evil 4 (2005) on the PS2 is the *Resident Evil* game that has most delighted (and terrified) critics. As of 26 Mar 2019, it had a scarily high rating of 95.85% from 54 reviews on GameRankings. "A non-stop thrill ride," said one review. "Players simply won't be able to stop and catch their breath."

SURVIVORS

MARCUS FENIX

Marcus Fenix and his fellow Gears have defended humanity from the fearsome Locust Horde over five missions and counting. Xbox gamers hold their backs-to-the-wall adventures just as sacred as those of the Master Chief in *Halo*.

1 HR 55 MIN 4 SEC

The **fastest completion of *Gears of War: Ultimate Edition*** was achieved by "Krinik". On 17 Apr 2019, the US gamer completed Microsoft's 2015 release in 1 hr 55 min 4 sec, as verified by Speedrun. The game's Roadie Run – a heads-down, weapons-ready sprint – is a godsend for speed-runners looking to charge through the game (or just run away from something BIG).

LOVE STORY

Despite the death and destruction all around, the love that Anya Stroud has for Marcus has never wavered. Even when Fenix was in jail, the strategist-turned-frontline-soldier vowed to fight for his release. Little wonder colleagues look to her as a rock of stability.

First board game based on a third-person-shooter videogame

Gears of War: The Board Game is a surprisingly faithful adaptation of Marcus's exploits. Designed by Corey Konieczka and published by Fantasy Flight, the 2011 game lets 1–4 players work together (or alone) to drive the Locust back to their holes.

Most expensive *Gears of War* collectable

To coincide with the release of *Gears of War 2* in 2008, the New York-based company TriForce Sales produced a 1:1 scale replica of a Lancer Assault Rifle. Only 300 of the 93-cm-long (37-in) models were made, each priced at $950 (£598).

Most viewed *Gears of War* video on YouTube

As of 22 Mar 2018, the "Gears of War (Mad World)" teaser for the original *Gears* had been viewed 12,777,511 times on YouTube. It was first uploaded on 3 Nov 2006.

Most critically acclaimed *Gears of War* videogame

The original – and still the best. As of 22 Mar 2019, *Gears of War* from 2006 remains the top-scoring game in the series. Released on Xbox 360, it averages 93.97% across 108 reviews, as verified by GameRankings. One reviewer praised the game's "timeless quality that keeps you coming back for more". This is perhaps why Microsoft chose to remaster and re-release the title in 2015 as *Gears of War: Ultimate Edition*.

SUPPORTING CAST

Only the toughest of the tough are selected to serve in the forces of the Coalition of Ordered Governments (COG for short).

Adam Fenix

Rarely sees eye to eye with son Marcus.

Dominic Santiago

Considers Marcus to be a brother.

Augustus Cole

Thrashball star now called the "Cole Train".

Samantha Byrne

On the frontline in the final battle at Azura.

JD Fenix

Marcus's son. Is he in the right line of work?

BEST-SELLING *GEARS OF WAR* GAME

Although the original *Gears of War* is the critical darling (see below far left), the entry that has sold the most copies is *Gears of War 2*. Released on 7 Nov 2008, it had shifted 6.75 million units as of 22 Mar 2019, according to VGChartz. Not that the other games in the series have been disappointments. *Gears of War* (2006) sold 6.09 million, while the third instalment helped itself to 6.22 million sales. These three Xbox exclusives all hit the target, enabling Microsoft's Xbox 360 console to compete successfully with Sony's PS3.

NEXT APPEARANCE

There's a new name to add to the *Gears of War* heroes listed left – Kait Diaz, who takes the lead in *Gears 5* as a soldier haunted by her past. Of course, Marcus will still be in the mix somewhere, with his inclusion already revealed by an official trailer.

115

CHOSEN UNDEAD

The Chosen Undead is *Dark Souls*' fated champion, destined to rise from the grave and ring the Bells of Awakening in Lordran. What the prophecy doesn't mention is that making the pilgrimage to Lordran is so very, very hard!

Death maps

On 4 Mar 2018, the hacker and PC gamer "DriftItem" worked out how to access network data in *Dark Souls* (Bandai Namco, 2011). This allowed him to convert thousands of bloodstain and soapstone message locations into maps that plotted precisely where players had died or left messages across many levels.

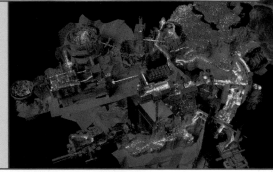

NEMESIS

Once you've fought your way past a sword-wielding wolf, a multiple-headed water beast and a stomach-turning dragon, Gwyn, Lord of Cinder still awaits. Don't let his aged appearance blind you to his great speed.

Dressed to kill

Twitch streamer "m_d_c_t" (aka Stephen LaFlamme) took immersive gaming to new levels when he became the **first to finish *Dark Souls II* wearing a real suit of armour**. The suit's weight and its restrictions on movement meant he played in 3–6-hr stints, finishing the 2014 game on 15 Oct 2018.

WEAPON SELECT

Just the names of these fearsome implements is enough to make the blood run cold. Each weapon rates highly when it comes to inflicting maximum damage in the shortest amount of time. But beware – even with one of these, *Dark Souls* is far from easy.

Zweihander

Uchigatana

Gravelord Sword

£3,771,474

Steamforged Games (UK) set itself a modest funding goal of £50,000 ($71,000) for *Dark Souls – The Board Game*. It took a reported three minutes to reach it! In total, 31,178 backers raised £3,771,474 ($5,413,840) from 19 Apr to 16 May 2016 – the **most money pledged to a Kickstarter board game based on a videogame.**

4,247 INVASIONS

Xbox One warrior "one4art" cut a swathe through other gamers to achieve the **most successful invasions in *Dark Souls: Remastered***. As of 4 Mar 2019, "one4art" had invaded the worlds of 4,247 hapless players in the 2018 remaster, leaving only when the doomed owner of the invaded world had been put to the sword.

FIRST NO-HIT COMPLETION OF *DARK SOULS: REMASTERED*

Bandai Namco's HD remaster of *Dark Souls* was so faithful to the original that veterans had no problem in surviving its formidable difficulty. On 24 May 2018, less than 24 hours after its release, UK Twitch streamer "The Happy Hob" completed a run-through in which the Chosen Undead emerged unscathed and completely untouched. His no-hit run took just over three-and-a-half hours.

Claws

Demon's Greataxe

Black Knight Greataxe

Gargoyle's Halberd

SNAPSHOT 📷

Dark Souls is tough – really tough – but it isn't until you encounter the Bell Gargoyles on the roof of the Undead Parish that you realize it's also evil! The first gargoyle you face is difficult enough, but soon its friend turns up to double the trouble. Together, the two make a formidable pairing that only the most skilled players will survive.

Largest single *Dark Souls* gameplay mod

The 403.2-MB *Dark Souls: Daughters of Ash* mod by "Grimrukh" was the largest fan-made expansion of *Dark Souls,* as of 22 Jan 2019. It's compatible with the *Prepare to Die Edition* on PC and offers new areas to explore and even more deadly foes to defeat.

117

ELLIE & JOEL

Whether the pair are laughing, crying, reminiscing about the past or just running for their lives, it's the father-daughter-like relationship between Ellie and Joel that's at the heart of what has made Sony's *The Last of Us* such a special survival-horror series.

LOVE STORY

The 2014 DLC prequel *The Last of Us: Left Behind* was a coming-of-age story focusing on the friendship – as well as the blossoming romance – between Ellie and Riley. But as the pair know only too well, heartbreak in the acclaimed game's post-apocalyptic world is only ever a bite away…

5,646,805 VIEWS

"LEGO® The Last of Us" is the **most watched *The Last of Us* fan film**. Described by creator Brian Anderson as "The Last of Us… but, you know, for kids!", it had notched up a total of 5,646,805 views as of 26 Mar 2019. In the 3-min video, LEGO versions of Joel and Ellie face-off against clickers, just as the pair do in the game.

Rarest *The Last of Us Remastered* multiplayer trophy

As of 1 Apr 2019, only 2% of players had earned the "Firefly" trophy. To earn this achievement, gamers must complete 84 online matches while playing as the Firefly faction.

A starring role

On 12 Mar 2014, actress Ashley Johnson (USA) became the **first female to receive a BAFTA Games Award for best performer**. It was for her portrayal of Ellie. She took the same award the next year, for *The Last of Us: Left Behind*.

2 HR 29 MIN 30 SEC

On 25 Apr 2019, America's "AnthonyCaliber" set the **fastest any% completion of *The Last of Us* on New Game Plus**, as verified by Speedrun. To get such a quick time means being very accurate with a sniper rifle while in the Suburbs area, and being as efficient as possible when using Molotov cocktails.

SUPPORTING CAST

In a devastated world, not many people are left. But the rich storytelling in *The Last of Us* means that you won't easily forget the people you do meet.

Marlene

Does the Fireflies' leader have a hidden agenda?

Tess

Smuggler who often works with Joel.

Tommy

Has fallen out of touch with brother Joel.

Henry & Sam

Siblings to whom survival is everything.

Riley

Ellie's best childhood friend and her first love.

QUICK FACT: The *Cordyceps* fungus that has infected the world in *The Last of Us* is real, but its zombifying poison works only on ants. Thank goodness!

MOST AWARDS WON BY A SURVIVAL-HORROR VIDEOGAME

Taking 140 awards from 220 nominations, *The Last of Us* (Sony, 2013) is the most decorated survival-horror game. Its excellence has been recognized in almost every award category, from the big one – game of the year – to technical achievement, story and individual character portrayals (see left). With a sequel getting ever closer, the series' domination is likely to continue...

NEXT APPEARANCE

The trailers released so far have already revealed some interesting tidbits from *The Last of Us Part II* – not least that Ellie and Joel appear to be estranged following the dramatic events of the previous game. Whatever happens, we're expecting plenty of exhilarating action, intriguing plot twists and no shortage of suffering.

KAZUMA KIRYU

When violence breaks out in Tokyo's criminal underworld, Kazuma's usually at the centre of it. He's happy to let his fists do the talking, so it's a good job the *Yakuza* star also happens to be one of the toughest characters to appear on a PlayStation.

First *Yakuza* game on a non-Sony console

Yakuza is usually associated with Sony's PlayStation, but it has appeared on another company's console. In 2013, a remaster of the first two games, *Ryū ga Gotoku 1&2 HD for Wii U*, appeared on Nintendo's device. As of 14 Mar 2019, the Japan-only title is the sole *Yakuza* title on anything other than a PlayStation.

1.5%

The **rarest non-Platinum trophy in *Yakuza 3*** is Minigame Master. As of 14 Mar 2019, only 1.5% of players had unlocked it. The trophy is awarded to those who complete every minigame. These include pool, darts, karaoke, bowling and more.

Most licensed Sega arcade games in a *Yakuza* title

Kazuma has his pick of Sega games to play in his spare time. In *Yakuza 6*, there are six: *Hang-On*, *OutRun* (above), *Puyo Puyo*, *Fantasy Zone*, *Space Harrier* and *Virtua Fighter 5*.

SUPPORTING CAST

In the *Yakuza* series, Tokyo's criminal underworld is full of dark deeds and shady personalities. To these people, life can be very cheap. As we make the introductions to some of the characters in Kazuma Kiryu's life, be careful not to tread on any toes!

Toru Hirose
Has the air of a wise old man, but he'll turn to violence at a moment's notice.

Takumi Someya
His snappy sense of style is just as sharp as his sword.

NEMESIS ☠

The villains you recall best always have a shred of humanity left. That's certainly true of Akira "Nishiki" Nishikiyama. Once, he was Kiryu's close friend, before a ruthless, murderous pursuit of power took hold. Is he now beyond saving?

12 TITLES

Kazuma's games usually gravitate around the fictional Tokyo district of Kamurocho (based on the real-life area of Kabukichō). It's featured in 12 titles, making it the **most recurring fictional Japanese district in games**. Different buildings might be open for business, but Kamurocho's neon lights are always on.

MOST UBIQUITOUS PS4 PROTAGONIST

The likes of Nathan Drake, Lara Croft and Kratos have all made repeated appearances on the PS4, but none can claim as many as Kazuma Kiryu. Since Sony's console launched in Nov 2013, he's the videogame character with the most starring roles. Taking both new titles and remasters of older games previously released on the PS3, the "Dragon of Dojima" has starred in eight PS4 games. His most recent outing was in *Yakuza 5* – a remaster of the classic PS3 title that came to the PS4 in Japan in Jun 2019.

Tsuyoshi Nagumo — This lieutenant of the Hirose Clan of Onomichi has a short fuse.

Yuta Usami — Behind his youthful appearance is a wild, self-destructive streak.

Kiyomi Kasahara — A voice of reason, but she has demons of her own to deal with.

LOVE STORY

Yumi Sawamura and Kazuma formed an intensely close bond as children. Since then, circumstances – not least Kazuma being imprisoned – have forced them apart. Absence has only made his heart grow fonder, but too much time might have passed for them to ever truly reconnect...

Most popular *Yakuza* videogame on Twitch

Yakuza 0 (Sega, 2015) tells the origin story of Kazuma Kiryu and how he came to be bound up with the Yakuza. It's the series' most popular game to watch on Twitch, with 100,338 people following its channel as of 14 Mar 2019. Could this be due to Kazuma's dance moves?

121

DANTE & NERO

Capcom's duo haven't always seen eye to eye, but in *Devil May Cry 5* they put their differences behind them to once more turn back the tides of Hell. Let the sword-swinging, gun-slinging, ultra-stylish demon-slaying commence.

NEMESIS

Mundus is a devil prince who ruled the Demon World 2,000 years ago. After being overthrown, he now has control of our world in his sights. Luckily for the humans, though, Dante and Nero are here to stop him.

First franchise crossover in a *Devil May Cry* videogame

Players who own the *Deluxe Edition* of *Devil May Cry 5* (2019) can clip Mega Man's famous Mega Buster to Nero's robotic arm. The gun works in a similar fashion to the way it operates when wielded by Mega Man: it can fire projectiles in rapid succession or be charged up to unleash a more devastating blast attack.

972,000 YEN

Japanese *Devil May Cry* fans with deep pockets could lay out 972,000 yen ($8,059; £6,626) for the *Dante Ultra Limited Edition* of *Devil May Cry 5*. At that price, it's not surprising that the package is the **most expensive collector's edition for an action-adventure game**. Owners receive a leather replica of Dante's coat (above). Other *Ultra Limited Editions* with Nero and V's jackets were sold for 810,000 yen ($7,253; £5,521) and 648,000 yen ($5,803; £4,417).

First Dante cameo in a *Monster Hunter* videogame

Dante has made many cameos (see opposite page). His first foray into the *Monster Hunter* series was in *Frontier G* (Capcom, 2013) as a freelancing Rasta who could fight alongside players – for a small payment, of course.

Fastest completion of *Devil May Cry* on "Dante Must Die!" difficulty

Enemies are more dangerous when playing with "Dante Must Die!" difficulty enabled. But on 3 Dec 2018, "Dasote" (JPN) defeated the 2001 game in 1 hr 0 min 30 sec, as verified by Speedrun.

WEAPON SELECT

Spilling demon blood is hard work. But Dante and Nero's weapons have been effective at averting Hell on Earth – so far...

Sparda

Dante's powerful sword was forged by demons.

Ebony & Ivory

Pistols infused with Dante's power.

Devil Breaker

Nero's customizable robotic arm.

Summoned Swords

Blades made of magical energy.

Yamato

A katana once wielded by Dante's father.

Rebellion

Dante's go-to blade throughout the series.

MOST UBIQUITOUS CAPCOM ACTION-ADVENTURE CHARACTER

A demon hunter's work is never done, as Dante (right) has found out. Since he hacked-and-slashed his way on to the scene in 2001, he has appeared in 25 games – seven *Devil May Cry* titles and 18 from other franchises. His cameos include roles in Capcom's *Viewtiful Joe* (2003), *SNK vs. Capcom: Card Fighters DS* (2006), *Marvel vs. Capcom 3: Fate of Two Worlds* (2011) and *Puzzle Fighter* (2017). It looks like Nero has plenty of catching up to do!

Fastest-selling *Devil May Cry* game

Speaking at the Game Developers Conference in San Francisco, California, USA, on 21 Mar 2019, Capcom's Hideaki Itsuno said that *Devil May Cry 5* had sold 2 million copies in just two weeks since its release on 8 Mar 2019. *Devil May Cry 4* sold *only* 3 million in its lifetime.

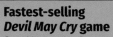

SNAPSHOT

Sparks fly when Dante and Nero first meet in *Devil May Cry 4* (2008). Not least because Nero's Devil Bringer has more than a few tricks up its sleeve – such as the ability to summon a powerful spectral arm (above).

123

STAR WARS

A VIDEOGAMES STORY

The best and worst Star Wars games are much like the heroes and villains from a galaxy far, far away. If they're good, they're very good. And if they're bad, they're awful...

1982
1992
1993
1993
1993

1994
1994
1995
1995
1996

LONGEST-RUNNING FILM LICENCE IN VIDEOGAMES

Since debuting with the Atari 2600 shooter Star Wars: The Empire Strikes Back in 1982, the Star Wars franchise has – appropriately enough – been a prolific force in videogaming. Almost every system has hosted a game based on the famous franchise and, with the 2019 release of EA's Star Wars Jedi: Fallen Order, the Star Wars licence will have been active and prolific for 37 years!

Here, we've rounded up some of the best and worst Star Wars games to be released over the years. The colour and intensity of their glow indicates their average review score on GameRankings.

LIGHT SIDE | RATING

MOST ACCLAIMED

Best-selling Star Wars game
Despite making its debut over 12 years ago,
LEGO® Star Wars: The Complete Saga
(LucasArts, 2007) remains the best-selling
Star Wars game with 15.33 million copies
sold, according to VGChartz.

RATING — DARK SIDE

MOST CRITICIZED ──────────➤

SECRET AGENTS

Keeping to the shadows or hiding in plain sight, these stealthy infiltrators are experts at remaining undetected. But if their cover is blown, they also have the skills to leave no witnesses.

Fastest time to complete the "Mark 'The Undying' Faba" contract in *Hitman 2*

Sean Bean has played many doomed characters, from *The Lord of the Rings*' Boromir to *Game of Thrones*' Ned Stark. IO Interactive and Warner Bros. decided to take this trend a step further by having him play a dead man walking in 2018's *Hitman 2* (main image).

Mark "The Undying" Faba, whose voice was provided by Bean, was introduced as the game's first Elusive Target on 20 Nov 2018. The two-week event granted players just one attempt to "take care" of Faba. IO Interactive confirmed that the fastest agent to kill Faba was Brazil's "Mendietinha" (aka Lucas Larini Kidricki, right), who did the deed in just 38 sec on 30 Nov 2018. He didn't even need his explosive Pale Duck (see pp.128–29).

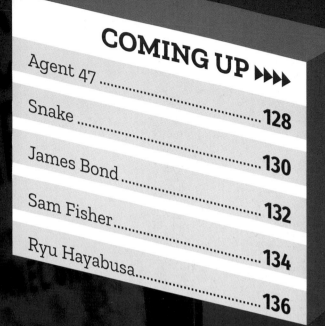

COMING UP ▶▶▶▶

AGENT 47

In the *Hitman* series, Agent 47 is a clone with a number instead of a name. The iconic, bald-headed assassin was created for a single deadly purpose – and it just so happens that he's really, really good at his job...

NEMESIS

Otto Wolfgang Ort-Meyer is the man behind the making of Agent 47. Through his cruelty and manipulation, he moulded his creation into the ultimate killing machine. But – as they say – what goes around comes around...

A hitman for all seasons

Agent 47's 2016 reboot, simply called *Hitman*, was the **first episodically released stealth-action game**. It was published digitally, with Square Enix putting out the title in six chapters between 11 Mar and 31 Oct 2016. The entire season was then given a physical release on 31 Jan 2017.

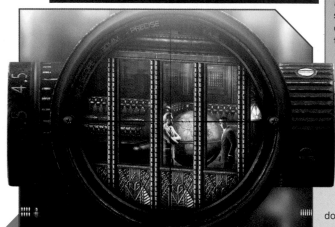

Fastest all-kills stealth completion of *Hitman: Sniper Challenge*

On 1 Feb 2019, Israel's "Markon" completed Square Enix's 2012 mini-game in 59.39 sec. That was impressive enough, but the sharpshooter did it while eliminating every target and remaining undetected. Agent 47 could hardly have done it any better himself.

WEAPON SELECT

Firearms are Agent 47's stock-in-trade, but the experienced super-assassin knows that some situations require a quieter – or altogether more radical – approach. Here, we take a look at some of the subtler ways in which he can "take care" of his targets.

Fiber Wire
A silent killer – one of Agent 47's favoured methods.

Emetic Pills
Foes will be sick to death of you after a couple of these.

On the big screen

Hitman (2007), starring Timothy Olyphant, is the **most critically acclaimed *Hitman* movie adaptation**. But scoring an average of just 35% from 22 reviews on Metacritic, that's not saying much...
Hitman: Agent 47 (2015), with Rupert Friend (right), fared even worse, scoring a meagre 28%.

SNAPSHOT

The first target that players had to eliminate as Agent 47 was Red Dragon Triad leader Lee Hong. Eidos' *Hitman: Codename 47* (2000) wasted no time in letting gamers find multiple ways to achieve their objective. One method was to take out Hong's limo driver, change into his uniform (left) and simply place an explosive in the vehicle. Job done.

MOST MISSIONS COMPLETED WITH FIVE STARS IN *HITMAN 2*

In Warner Bros.' stealthy 2018 thriller, Agent 47's contracts are graded out of five. Players are scored on the time taken, the number of non-target casualties and whether they remained undetected. As of 5 Mar 2019, the Xbox One player with the most flawless missions was "SpirantCrayon22", who had earned 247 five-star ratings. The nearest rival to this lethal perfectionist was the UK's "Euler13", with 119.

Briefcase

Carry this disguised explosive just about anywhere.

Shovel

One of many impromptu weapons at Agent 47's disposal.

The Pale Duck

Expect a bang at bathtime with this rubber ducky.

First stealth-action videogame protagonist to assassinate himself

In the *Hitman: Codename 47* mission "Meet Your Brother", Agent 47 has to face off against an army of himself. The "Subject 48" clones all share his skill with a weapon. But thankfully for 47, they don't have the wealth of experience he's earned outside the lab.

4.28 MILLION

Keen to make a killing on the sales of *Hitman: Codename 47*, Eidos gave IO Interactive (the game's developer) two years to make a sequel. *Hitman 2: Silent Assassin* didn't disappoint. After its release on 1 Oct 2002, it went on to be the **best-selling** *Hitman* **game**. As of 5 Mar 2019, it had sold 4.28 million copies, as verified by VGChartz.

SNAKE

As all *Metal Gear* fans will know, there's more than one Snake who takes centre stage in the series' games. But no matter whether you're playing as Naked Snake, Solid Snake or Venom Snake, the key to success is to sneak.

BIG DEBUT

Solid Snake starred in 1987's *Metal Gear* – the series' start for the MSX2 home computer.

SNAPSHOT 📷

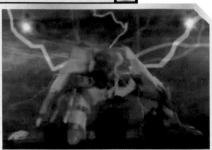

The intro to *Metal Gear Solid 2: Sons of Liberty* (2001) is among gaming's best. Hidden by stealth tech, Snake leaps on board a ship from a nearby bridge. But the landing and the rain break his sneaking suit, causing sparks to fly (above).

First *Metal Gear* game to provide an in-game clue on its box

Metal Gear has encouraged players to think outside the box from the start, but with *Metal Gear 2: Solid Snake* (1990) for the MSX2, they had to literally *look* at the box. On the back was a radio frequency that Snake had to call in-game in order to bypass the title's copy protection. *Metal Gear Solid* (1998) for the PSOne famously included a similar image on its own box.

Fastest completion of *Metal Gear Solid: The Twin Snakes*

Konami's 2004 remake of *Metal Gear Solid* for the Nintendo GameCube still fascinates many speed-runners. The fastest "Normal" difficulty run was achieved by the USA's "Aerlien", who flew rather than sneaked through the action in just 54 min 34 sec on 11 Aug 2018, as verified by Speedrun.

BOSS FIGHT

The members of this rogues' gallery of bad guys and girls from 1998's *Metal Gear Solid* all pose different life-threatening challenges to Snake. Most also force players to challenge their approach – by selecting the right weapon or by unplugging the control pad...

Few enemies are quicker on the draw in a gunfight.

Revolver Ocelot

Cyborg Ninja

Only fisticuffs will do when confronting this ghostly ninja.

First tactical espionage game to allow pacifist completion

Metal Gear Solid 3 (2004) was the first stealth game in which it was possible to complete all missions, including boss encounters, by using non-lethal force. Naked Snake may tranquilize his antagonists or, in one boss's case, wait for them to die of old age.

NEXT APPEARANCE

With Snake not present during the events of 2018's *Metal Gear Survive*, and no new series entry within sight, his next appearance will be in a different breed of game. IDW Games and Konami have decided to roll the dice to co-create a tabletop version, due in 2019. *Metal Gear Solid: The Board Game* will follow the storyline of the 1998 PSOne classic.

130

MOST EXPENSIVE STEALTH GAME PRODUCED

Stealthy though Snake is, the fact that *Metal Gear Solid V: The Phantom Pain* cost Konami over $80 million (£51.9 million) to develop is no secret. *The Nikkei*, a Japanese business newspaper, reported the figure a month before the game launched in Sep 2015. This, in addition to the necessary marketing spend, encouraged gaming sites and business wires to speculate upon how many units would need to be sold to break even. It shifted over six million – more than enough.

Psycho Mantis

This psychic will dodge Snake's attacks. Time for drastic measures!

Sniper Wolf

She tracks her prey with infinite patience and never misses.

Liquid Snake

The brother of Solid Snake, but with none of his heroic intent.

First non-Nintendo characters in a *Super Smash Bros.* game

The inclusion of Snake in *Super Smash Bros. Brawl* (2008) was an unexpected treat for fans of Konami's sneak-'em-up. Snake's big moment was shared by Sonic the Hedgehog, who also stepped into Nintendo's fighting game.

Best-selling stealth videogame series

For characters who prefer to stay in the shadows, Solid Snake and co. have hogged plenty of the limelight. In a statement on 31 Mar 2018, Konami confirmed that cumulative worldwide sales of the *Metal Gear* series had exceeded 53.8 million copies following the release of *Metal Gear Survive* in Feb 2018.

JAMES BOND

We've been expecting you, Mister Bond. The suave super-spy is armed with his famous licence to kill and he's used it in top-secret missions for Queen and country across the gaming world, as well as on the big screen.

"DON'T MOVE, MR. BOND! GIVE ME THAT ENVELOPE..."

Most James Bond films adapted in a single videogame
Activision's *007 Legends* (2012) was based on six films: *Goldfinger* (1964), *On Her Majesty's Secret Service* (1969), *Moonraker* (1979, featuring Jaws, above), *Licence to Kill* (1989), *Die Another Day* (2002) and *Skyfall* (2012).

First point-and-click James Bond game
Bond's outings are usually action heavy, but *James Bond 007: The Stealth Affair* (Interplay, 1990) was a point-and-click adventure game. Licensing rights meant Bond starred in the US version only. Elsewhere, it was branded *Operation Stealth* (US Gold), with 007 replaced by CIA agent John Glames.

Most prolific publisher of 007 games
The UK's most glamorous secret agent inspired EA to publish a total of 10 James Bond-themed games between 1999 and 2005. In *GoldenEye: Rogue Agent* (2004), the player controls an MI6 agent kicked out of the service rather than 007 himself. The **first James Bond game** was *Shaken but Not Stirred* (Richard Shepherd Software), a text adventure released in 1982.

The four-way multiplayer in 1997's *GoldenEye 007* wasn't just a shock for gamers. The story goes that even senior management at Rare were kept in the dark as the production team designed the ground-breaking deathmatch mode.

First movie-based 007 game
Bond has been saving the world in games since 1982, but it wasn't until *James Bond 007: A View to a Kill* (Mindscape) and *A View to a Kill: The Computer Game* (Domark) that a 007 movie adaptation was sanctioned. Both games launched on 13 Jun 1985 to coincide with the film's cinematic release.

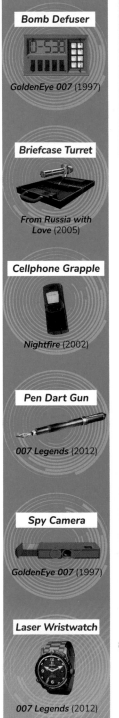

WEAPON SELECT
"Q" branch always makes sure that Bond goes into the field with more than just his tuxedo and charm. Here are some of his accessories and the 007 games they first appeared in.

Bomb Defuser
GoldenEye 007 (1997)

Briefcase Turret
From Russia with Love (2005)

Cellphone Grapple
Nightfire (2002)

Pen Dart Gun
007 Legends (2012)

Spy Camera
GoldenEye 007 (1997)

Laser Wristwatch
007 Legends (2012)

NEMESIS

Criminal mastermind Ernst Stavro Blofeld has been a regular – and sadistic – presence in Bond's movies. But he appears only twice in 007 games – in *GoldenEye: Rogue Agent* (EA, 2004) and *007 Legends* (Activision, 2012).

Best-selling James Bond videogame

Connery or Moore? Craig or Brosnan? The debate about the best screen Bond goes on, but there's no doubt about the most popular 007 game. As of 13 Feb 2019, *GoldenEye 007* (Nintendo, 1997) for the N64 had sold 8.09 million copies worldwide, according to VGChartz.

FASTEST COMPLETION OF *GOLDENEYE 007*

More than 20 years after its first release, speed-runners are still taking on the N64's *GoldenEye 007* (1997) with a view to leaving their rivals very much shaken and stirred. On 22 May 2018, Danish gamer "Marc" thunder(ball)ed his way through the Nintendo-published but Rare-developed first-person shooter on "Agent" difficulty in 21 min 43 sec. His record was added to Speedrun and verified on 2 Oct 2018. That shaved nine seconds off the previous best time of 21 min 52 sec, set by Pakistan's "Ace", which had stood for almost five years.

SAM FISHER

The *Splinter Cell* special-ops agent has been the scourge of bad guys since his debut in 2002. Imagine the sheer horror of seeing those three green lights turn their attention towards you – it's *almost* enough to make you feel sorry for the criminals.

EIGHT WEEKS

Other gaming franchises have transitioned well into print, but few have been as successful as the *Splinter Cell* books. *Tom Clancy's Splinter Cell: Conviction* (2009) has the **most weeks on *The New York Times* Best Sellers list for a game novelization** – eight.

First game concept to become real-world hardware?

Legend has it that Tom Clancy initially rejected Ubisoft's design for Fisher's famous trifocal goggles as he felt the tech was unlikely to see the light of day. Little did he know that, in 2004, a US tech outfit would launch a system with similar looks and capabilities.

First videogame to feature a fully stealth-based co-op mode

Ubisoft's *Splinter Cell: Chaos Theory* (2005) incorporates fully fledged stealth-focused gameplay into its co-op mode. Two rookie Third Echelon agents – creatively called Agent One and Agent Two – are dropped into seven purpose-built standalone missions that encourage teamwork throughout.

WEAPON SELECT

Few accessorize better than Sam Fisher. He has enough gadgets and gizmos to make even James Bond go back to "Q" branch and ask for a better deal.

Trifocal Goggles
See the bad guys without being seen on night-time operations.

Optic Cable
Spy on enemies from a discreet – and safe – distance.

Tri-Rotor
Get vital intel on the opposition with this spy drone.

SNAPSHOT 📷

Sam Fisher's party trick for avoiding detection – one that we don't recommend trying at home – is doing the splits to support himself between walls. The move proved a hit with gamers when they first saw it in *Tom Clancy's Splinter Cell* (2002). Since then, it has become something of a trademark. It's a good job that bad guys never look up!

First Sam Fisher cameo

It took 16 years for Sam to appear in a game not in the *Splinter Cell* franchise. On 10 Apr 2018, he was plunged into *Tom Clancy's Ghost Recon: Wildlands* (Ubisoft, 2017) in a DLC mission entitled "Special Operation 1: Splinter Cell". During the cameo, Sam even laments the demise of the stealth genre.

MOST MARTIAL ART STYLES USED IN ONE GAME

In order to make Sam Fisher as badass as possible, Ubisoft consulted with Kevin Secours – the founder of Integrated Fighting Systems and director of the International Combat Systema Association – during the development of *Splinter Cell: Blacklist* (2013). Secours suggested they furnish Fisher with eight techniques: the Russian martial art of systema, plus jujitsu, kali, silat, kung fu, muay Thai and general law-enforcement and defensive tactics. Fisher's new knife, his Indonesian karambit, was also recommended by Secours.

Tactical Audio Kit
Eavesdrop on top-secret conversations using this laser-based mic.

Camera Jammer
Never get caught on camera with this handheld surveillance disruptor.

Sticky Camera
This handy camera can be placed just about anywhere.

NEXT APPEARANCE

Sam Fisher's cameo in *Ghost Recon: Wildlands* (left) has fuelled rumours that a new *Splinter Cell* game is in development. It's something that hasn't been quelled by *Far Cry: New Dawn* (Ubisoft, 2019) containing Sam's suit. No doubt all will be revealed at E3 2019 during one of the press conferences by Ubisoft or Microsoft. Stay tuned.

59 MIN 32 SEC

The fast-flowing, non-stop action of *Splinter Cell: Conviction* (2010) was a bid by Ubisoft to push its stealth series in a new direction. Unsurprisingly, the formula was a hit with speed-runners. On 22 Jul 2018, PC player "FaceKillerPanda" (UK) set the **fastest time to complete Conviction** at 59 min 32 sec, as verified by Speedrun.

135

RYU HAYABUSA

Deadly and stealthy in equal measure, Tecmo's ninja has been slinking through the shadows since the 1980s. The *Ninja Gaiden* games are famed for their difficulty, but Ryu – half-man, half-demon – has the strength to take on all comers.

First console game to use narrative cutscenes

The idea of games having a back story started to take shape in 1988, when *Ninja Gaiden* (Tecmo) was ported from the arcade to the Famicom. The first in-game cutscene was a short animated sequence that revealed the fate of Ryu's father and gave our hero the emotional drive to exact revenge.

Most reworked versions of a hack-and-slash videogame

Ryu's first foray into 3D in *Ninja Gaiden* (2004) has been honed to a razor-sharp edge over the years. No fewer than four reworkings have been created, most recently the Xbox One X version of *Ninja Gaiden Black* on 24 Oct 2017.

BOSS FIGHT

When Tecmo re-imagined *Ninja Gaiden* in 2004, it took the opportunity to create some of the toughest bosses gamers had ever faced. Here is just a selection of the extraordinary enemies from Ryu Hayabusa's classic hack-and-slash adventure.

This mounted samurai takes Ryu to task in the first act.

Masakado

Doku

The Lord of the Greater Fiends is lethal in battle.

NEMESIS ☠

Jaquio is a demonic sorcerer that torments Ryu in the early NES *Ninja Gaiden* games. His intent is to throw the gates of Hell wide open as he unleashes unspeakable demonic forces on the world. Luckily, there's a ninja for that.

Fastest completion of *Ninja Gaiden* (NES)

The fiendish difficulty of Ryu's maiden outing in *Ninja Gaiden* keeps on enticing speed-runners. The USA's "Arcus" took just 11 min 38 sec to tear through the game, as verified on 13 Jun 2018 by Speedrun. It included Stage 6-2, with some of gaming's hardest platforming sections.

MOST UBIQUITOUS VIDEOGAME NINJA

By their nature, you never know a ninja's whereabouts. All you can be certain of is that Ryu will appear when he's needed the most. As of 1 Mar 2019, Hayabusa had appeared in 37 titles. The first was in 1988's original *Ninja Gaiden* arcade game (below left), while the most recent – 31 years later – was his regular series cameo in 2019's *Dead or Alive 6* (below right). He even made a playable appearance in Koei Tecmo's *Warriors Orochi 3* in 2011.

Marbus
This flying demon's fireballs rain down from above, so move!

Alma
An innocent girl turned into a Greater Fiend by Doku.

Vigoor Emperor
Seemingly immortal tyrant with unlimited powers.

Most critically acclaimed *Ninja Gaiden* videogame

Of all Ryu's games, it's *Ninja Gaiden Black* (2005) that silently slips in ahead of the rest in terms of review ratings. As of 8 Feb 2019, it averaged 94.76% across 38 GameRankings reviews. "The most exciting, frenetic and rewarding gaming experience in recent memory," said one.

LOVE STORY

Irene Lew is as headstrong as Ryu – so much so that she ignores an order from her CIA bosses to kill Ryu, instead helping him escape after the events of 1988's *Ninja Gaiden*. Romance blooms between the two just before the end credits roll.

137

e-sports
MVPs

Faker
Pro since 2013

WINS
14

REAL NAME: Lee Sang-hyeok (KOR)
MVP in... *League of Legends* (Riot Games, 2009)
TOTAL EARNINGS: $1,175,927 (£911,655)

Gesture
Pro since 2017

WINS
5

REAL NAME: Hong Jae-hee (KOR)
MVP in... *Overwatch* (Blizzard, 2016)
TOTAL EARNINGS: $194,730 (£150,967)

KuroKy
Pro since 2008

WINS
39

REAL NAME: Kuro Takhasomi (DEU)
MVP in... *DOTA 2* (Valve, 2013)
TOTAL EARNINGS: $4,135,203 (£3,205,880)

NuckleDu
Pro since 2012

WINS
7

REAL NAME: Du Cong Dang (USA)
MVP in... *Street Fighter V* (Capcom, 2016)
TOTAL EARNINGS: $304,673 (£236,202)

SonicFox
Pro since 2013

WINS
4

REAL NAME: Dominique McLean (USA)
MVP in... *Dragon Ball FighterZ* (Bandai Namco, 2018)
TOTAL EARNINGS: $28,497 (£22,092)

TekKz
Pro since 2018

WINS
3

REAL NAME: Donovan Hunt (UK)
MVP in... *FIFA 19* (EA, 2018)
TOTAL EARNINGS: $107,000 (£82,953)

In our special sticker book of e-sports champions, we've brought together the highest-earning pro players from 12 hugely popular competitive games. These are the most valuable players (MVPs) in the most literal of senses, and they make their living doing what we all love – playing videogames!

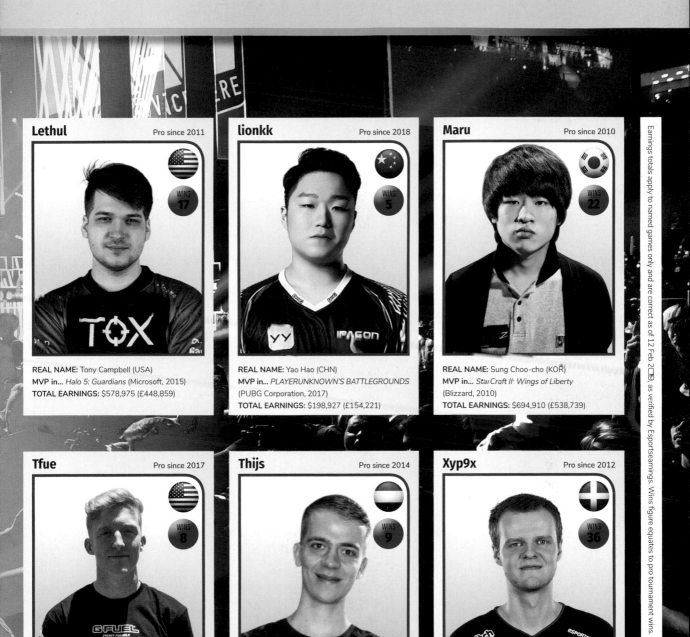

Lethul
Pro since 2011

WINS **17**

REAL NAME: Tony Campbell (USA)
MVP in... *Halo 5: Guardians* (Microsoft, 2015)
TOTAL EARNINGS: $578,975 (£448,859)

lionkk
Pro since 2018

WINS **5**

REAL NAME: Yao Hao (CHN)
MVP in... *PLAYERUNKNOWN'S BATTLEGROUNDS* (PUBG Corporation, 2017)
TOTAL EARNINGS: $198,927 (£154,221)

Maru
Pro since 2010

WINS **22**

REAL NAME: Sung Choo-cho (KOR)
MVP in... *StarCraft II: Wings of Liberty* (Blizzard, 2010)
TOTAL EARNINGS: $694,910 (£538,739)

Tfue
Pro since 2017

WINS **8**

REAL NAME: Turner Tenney (USA)
MVP in... *Fortnite Battle Royale* (Epic, 2017)
TOTAL EARNINGS: $463,800 (£359,568)

Thijs
Pro since 2014

WINS **9**

REAL NAME: Thijs Molendijk (NLD)
MVP in... *Hearthstone* (Blizzard, 2014)
TOTAL EARNINGS: $418,839 (£324,711)

Xyp9x
Pro since 2012

WINS **36**

REAL NAME: Andreas Højsleth (DNK)
MVP in... *Counter-Strike: Global Offensive* (Valve, 2012)
TOTAL EARNINGS: $1,321,921 (£1,024,840)

Earnings totals apply to named games only and are correct as of 12 Feb 2019, as verified by Esportsearnings. Wins figure equates to pro tournament wins.

SPEEDRUN.COM

Whoosh! That's the sound of a speed-runner setting another record. In a chapter produced in partnership with Speedrun.com, you'll meet the gamers with the fastest fingers and the sharpest reactions.

Most speed-run game of 2018

The intricate level design and tight controls in Matt Makes Games' *Celeste* (2018) have proven particularly popular with speed-runners. From its release on 25 Jan 2018 to the end of the year, 4,840 runs had been uploaded to Speedrun's servers. That was more even than last year's most speed-run game, *Super Mario Odyssey* (4,265 runs in 2018), and *Super Mario 64* (3,276), with Mario's titles relegated to the silver and bronze positions on Speedrun's podium.

COMING UP ▶▶▶▶

GWR ON SPEEDRUN

Ever wanted to have a go at setting the fastest speedrun in your favourite game, but didn't know where to start? Wonder no more. This year, we're introducing GWR-made speedruns to Speedrun.com itself – read on for all the exciting details...

Sprinting on to Speedrun.com

In recent years, Guinness World Records has been working ever closer with Speedrun.com. Not only is the website an authority on all the speedrun records we include in the book, it's also where we source the facts and figures that go into this very chapter.

This year, we're delighted to announce that we've made it an official partnership. If you visit **www.speedrun.com**, you'll see that there's now a GWR section populated with speedruns from the latest games. Any of you can try to beat the existing benchmarks you'll find there. To attempt one of these challenges, all you have to do is sign up as a Speedrun.com member. Simply visit the website, click "Sign up" and enter your details.

GWR's challenges aren't your traditional runs. Instead of asking you to complete entire games, we've created bespoke runs that will have you aiming to complete specific and imaginative objectives against the clock.

Did you think defeating the Ruined Dragon was already a tough ask? Try taking the monster on against the clock!

The Trials of Muspelheim already give Kratos a headache, but completing them quickly adds a whole new level of complexity.

Grab a GWR certificate

For example, one of our *Super Mario Odyssey* challenges tasks players with winning all six boss rematches in the Mushroom Kingdom. Another involves vanquishing every wave of enemies that the fiery Muspelheim throws against Kratos in 2018's *God of War*.

Another difference between our speedruns and those on the rest of Speedrun.com is that we'll keep a close eye on them. If you're good enough to grab the top spot, make an application at **www.guinnessworldrecords.com** – be sure to supply the evidence we need (full details are on our website) – and we'll look to verify your claim. If successful, you can claim a GWR certificate!

New speedruns will be added each month, so be sure to check back regularly. And make sure you listen to our *Gamer's Podcast*, where we'll keep you up to date with the recently added runs, the fastest times and all the rest of the latest gaming news.

Q&A WITH PETER CHASE
Founder of Speedrun.com

What led you to start Speedrun.com?
In late 2013, there was a lot of talk about the need for a global speed-running leaderboard website. I started coding up a demo. Then, by working with the people in planning over at SpeedRunsLive.com, it was launched with their backing. Speedrun communities started to migrate over and Speedrun.com gradually became the main hub for speed-running.

How do you decide which games will be included on the site?
We have an approval process in place, where users can request a game to be added to the site. They must show a full completed speedrun they've done of the game. We currently have more than 15,000 games listed on the site!

How are speedruns verified?
Community figures from each game are appointed as moderators of that title. When a run is submitted, it requires verification from one of the moderators before it can appear on the leaderboard. Generally, they check to ensure the timer is accurate and that the gameplay is legitimate.

What advice do you have for gamers who want to start speed-running?
Play a game that you enjoy, because it takes a lot of motivation, practice and perseverance. Luckily, many games have speedrun tutorials available on YouTube, while communities are always willing to help out newcomers.

How excited are you to have a GWR section on Speedrun.com?
It will be great to have a new type of challenge available, and exciting for users to have their work recognized officially by Guinness World Records!

HOW TO FIND GWR'S CHALLENGES

1) Go to Speedrun.com
2) Click "More" in the top navigation bar
3) Click "GWR"

HIGHLIGHTS OF THE YEAR

The last 12 months have seen speed-runners provide us with a bonanza of spectacular new records. We've witnessed a "perfect" run in *Super Mario Bros.*, an all-but-unbeatable record falling in *Ultimate DOOM* and a host of times tumbling in other great games...

Super Mario Bros. (1985)

In a three-way battle of US gamers in *Super Mario Bros.* (Nintendo), it's "somewes" who's currently ahead. On 22 Oct 2018, the American set the **fastest time to complete** *Super Mario Bros.*, defeating Bowser in 4 min 55.796 sec. The record is thought to be close to the game's theoretical fastest time... not that this has put off his long-time rivals – "Kosmic" and "RoyLT" – from trying to top it.

Marvel's Spider-Man (2018)

Super-villains should watch out when "JHobz" pulls on Spidey's mask. As verified on 26 Feb 2019, the US gamer set the **fastest completion** in a spidey-sense-tingling 4 hr 11 min 36 sec to complete Sony's web-spinner on its hardest "Ultimate" difficulty mode on New Game Plus.

Baten Kaitos: Eternal Wings and the Lost Ocean (2003)

Sometimes, speed-runs don't seem very, well, speedy. A 100% run of *Baten Kaitos: Eternal Wings and the Lost Ocean* (Namco) took "Baffan" (FRA) 341 hr 20 min 3 sec in Dec 2016. This record for the **fastest completion** is still standing as of 29 Apr 2019! That is a *long* time, but it included the two weeks it takes for the "Shampoo" item to age into "Splendid Hair" – the final piece that speed-runners require for a 100% completion of the game.

Apex Legends (2019)

Players of *Titanfall* and *Titanfall 2* will know that both titles include a secret homage to the Loch Ness Monster ("Nessie"). Developer Respawn Entertainment repeated the trick in EA's *Apex Legends*. To make "Nessie" appear in the waters off the east coast of the map, players have to find and shoot the 10 plushies (right) scattered around the game's environment. The three-person team of "Pulsy"(BIH), "Nyomdalee"(CZE) and "TheCealianProphet" set the **fastest time to summon Nessie** on 23 Mar 2019, taking 3 min 39 sec.

The Legend of Zelda: Breath of the Wild (2017)

On 29 Jan 2019, Brazil's "SpecsNStats" took just 25 hr 24 min 57 sec to set the **fastest 100% completion of Breath of the Wild** (Nintendo). The run includes completing every shrine and side quest, visiting every tower, obtaining the Master Sword and finding all 900 of the hidden Koroks (left).

Resident Evil 2 (2019)

Those who are good enough at *Resident Evil 2* (Capcom) will eventually unlock "The Tofu Survivor" campaign. It's a mode that harks back to the original *Resident Evil 2* (1998), in which players were able to unlock a rectangular character (lovingly referred to as Tofu, right) that was used to test the game during its period of development. On 13 Apr 2019, "xXAlucard" (USA) set the **fastest time to complete "The Tofu Survivor" on PC**, running through in 7 min 17 sec.

Shovel Knight: Plague of Shadows (2015)

One of the many quirky aspects of *Shovel Knight* (Yacht Club Games) is that you can pet some of the furry friends you encounter on your travels. On 2 Feb 2018, "Tohloo" raced through *Plague of Shadows* to **set the fastest time to pet the Memmec** (above) – the Canadian took 3 min 8 sec to give the fox-like creature a friendly pat.

Ultimate DOOM (1995)

A speed-run that survives for 21 years is rare, but that was the case with the **fastest completion of the E1M1: Hangar level on Ultimate DOOM** (id Software). The time of 9 sec, set by "Panter" in 1998, stood for so long because *DOOM*'s in-game stopwatch rounds times up, so that even a time of 8.1 sec would show as 9 sec. The record finally fell on 23 Feb 2019, when the USA's "4shockblast" shaved it to 8 sec.

Anthem (2019)

The Heart of Rage in *Anthem* (EA) is a terrifying maelstrom that destroys entire cities and unleashes monstrosities. But that didn't deter one particular team of fearless speed-runners. The group, consisting of "dr33d_tv", "Icyhop3", "Kashanu" and "TraxXx540", fought their way through hordes of enemies to record the **fastest completion of the "Heart of Rage" stronghold** (on "Easy" difficulty) in 5 min 42 sec on 6 May 2019.

CO-OP SPEEDRUNS

Solo speed-runners have their destiny in their own hands, but that's not the case with co-op attempts. You have to work in perfect harmony with your fellow runners and resist the urge to be a glory hunter. Here are just a few of the great co-op runs on Speedrun.

Secret of Mana (1993)

Square's classic Super Nintendo RPG *Secret of Mana* is notable not only for being a fantastic game, but also for including a three-player mode. On 19 May 2017, speed-runners "Yagamoth" (CHE), "BOWIEtheHERO" (UK) and "StingerPA" (USA) teamed up to record the **fastest co-op completion** (and save the magical Mana Tree) in 1 hr 45 min 59 sec.

The Legend of Zelda: Tri Force Heroes (2015)

Three's the magic number in Nintendo's Link-laden 3DS adventure. On 4 Mar 2018, the trio of "Cognition_TV", "zed0" (both UK) and "TheImpasta" raced through the game's dungeons in 4 hr 17 min 1 sec to achieve the **fastest multiplayer completion**. Success seemed to take the trio by surprise, as they commented: "This was actually meant to be a practice."

A Way Out (2018)

EA's action-adventure follows framed banker Vincent and thief Leo as they hatch a plot to bust out of prison and then try to set the record straight. The Norwegian duo of "credogy" and "LanoKingen" worked in tandem as they achieved the **fastest co-op completion** in 3 hr 12 min 42 sec, as verified on 10 May 2018. They played online (rather than couch co-op) on the PC.

Left 4 Dead 2 (2009)

Surviving while facing wave after wave of zombies in Valve's *Left 4 Dead 2* requires slick and skilful teamwork at the best of times. But "TheMaster", "MrFailzz" (both USA), "mr.deagle" (CAN) and "bill_play3" (BRA) decided to take on the co-op shooter's undead hordes while playing through the game's most difficult "Expert Realism" mode. On 25 Feb 2018, the quartet achieved the **fastest main campaign co-op completion** in 52 min 8 sec. This involves blasting through the "Dead Center", "Dark Carnival", "Swamp Fever", "Hard Rain" and "The Parish" levels.

Portal 2 (2011)

It's mind-bending enough when you play it by yourself, but introduce another player – and another Portal Gun – into Valve's *Portal 2* and things really do get complicated. As verified on 26 Jan 2019, the crack team of "AJ" and "Betsruner" (both USA) teleported their way through *Portal 2*'s tests in 27 min 30.967 sec to set the **fastest all main courses co-op completion**.

Resident Evil 5 (2009)

With mutants and monsters roaming about in *Resident Evil 5*, it's just as well that Capcom's acclaimed survival-horror title allows players to cover each other's backs. Finnish gamers "JenzAmaka" and "sgtblack" paired up to complete the **fastest New Game+ co-op completion** (with "Professional" difficulty switched on) in 1 hr 17 min 47 sec on 28 Jan 2016.

Borderlands 2 (2012)

The world of Pandora in 2K Games' "looter shooter" isn't the kind of place you want to brave alone if you can help it. But the team of "amyrlinn", "Shockwve", "bisnap" (all USA) and "BlackfireSin" turned the tables on the game's monsters, robots and psychos to set the **fastest four-player completion**. The quartet stormed through the game's missions in 1 hr 37 min 56 sec on 21 Jan 2017.

Halo: Combat Evolved (2001)

"The Silent Cartographer", the fourth mission you'll face in *Halo: CE*, is arguably the most iconic mission in Microsoft's famous franchise. It opens with the Master Chief on board a dropship as it ferries him to the frontline. The level takes players seamlessly from huge outdoor warfare to claustrophobic corridors full of bad guys. On 6 Apr 2015, "Cocopuffs239" (USA) and "Daveofhyrule" sprinted past the beautiful scenery to set the **fastest co-op completion of "The Silent Cartographer" on "Easy" difficulty** in 3 min 34 sec.

TOP TIMES #1

Here we bring you the fastest times from the 50 games with the most-posted runs on Speedrun.com in Mar 2019 – for those who like to know, *Resident Evil 2* (2019) was the most popular that month. All records were correct as of 12 Apr 2019.

All times are presented in the format HH:MM:SS.

Cuphead
StudioMDHR's 2017 shmup is famous for its gorgeous animation, but speed-runners barely have time to take it in as they breeze through.

GAME	RUN TYPE	PLAYER	TIME	PLATFORM
Captain Toad: Treasure Tracker	Any%; Wii U	SingleScoop (USA)	01:18:35	Wii U
Cat Bird	Marda; Any%	Th3on3C (CAN)	00:04:47	Android
Celeste	Any%	TGH (USA)	00:27:52.052	PC
Club Penguin Rewritten	500 Coins; No Bonuses	Lothjon (DNK)	00:00:33.180	Web
Crash Bandicoot: N. Sane Trilogy	Crash Bandicoot; Any%	DepCow (USA)	00:42:19	PC
Cuphead	All Bosses; Regular; Legacy	SBDWolf (ITA)	00:23:25	PC
Diddy Kong Racing	100%	Obiyo (CAN)	01:47:38	N64
Garfield Kart	All Cups 50cc; PC	Divad (CAN)	00:37:15	PC
Getting Over It with Bennett Foddy	Glitchless	Stillow (SRB)	00:01:17.729	PC
Grand Theft Auto: Vice City	Any%	RoK_24 (DEU)	00:08:38	PC
Kingdom Hearts III	Any%; Beginner	SwiftShadow (USA)	02:45:50	PS4 Pro

Captain Toad: Treasure Tracker
The courses in Nintendo's 2014 puzzle-adventure are twisting, turning mazes. Speed-running the title becomes a memory test, with players having to remember the most direct routes.

Getting Over It with Bennett Foddy
One of the more bizarre titles to entice speed-runners (and YouTubers) is Bennett Foddy's indie game in which players have to scale a mountain with only a hammer for help.

Mario Kart 8 Deluxe

When you've won every grand prix and unlocked every hidden character in Nintendo's racer, you can always turn your attention to shaving milliseconds off your best times.

GAME	RUN TYPE	PLAYER	TIME	PLATFORM
The Legend of Zelda	Any% No Up+A; NES	lackattack24 (USA)	00:28:17	NES
The Legend of Zelda: A Link to the Past	No Major Glitches; Any%	Xelna (CAN)	01:23:10	SNES
The Legend of Zelda: Breath of the Wild	Any%; No amiibo	sketodara01417 (JPN)	00:29:16.6	Wii U
The Legend of Zelda: Majora's Mask	Any%	EnNopp112 (SWE)	01:15:59	Wii Virtual Console
The Legend of Zelda: Ocarina of Time	Any%	Torje (NOR)	00:17:01.566	Wii Virtual Console
LEGO® Star Wars: The Complete Saga	Any%; Solo	Binyour13 (USA)	01:09:05	PC
Luigi's Mansion: Dark Moon	Any%	RiiDOLSK (USA)	02:50:28	3DS
Mario Kart 8 Deluxe	Nitro Tracks; Items; 150cc	BrawlerJesse (USA)	00:40:28	Switch
Mario Kart Wii	32 Tracks; No Skips; No Items	VBarone99 (USA)	01:14:09	Wii
The Messenger	8-Bit; No OoB; New Game	KuningasEST (EST)	00:30:54	PC
Miles & Kilo	Any%	Kotslayer (DEU)	00:17:58.760	Switch
Monster Hunter World	Any%; 1 Player; Console	mosstkm (JPN)	05:18:28	PS4
New Super Mario Bros.	Any%; Official Releases	MoistenedWah (USA)	00:22:58.3	3DS

The Messenger

Devolver Digital's 2D action-platformer has made a big splash in the speed-running community since its 2018 release. To be the fastest ninja, you'll need absolute precision in every step, leap and swipe of your sword.

The Legend of Zelda

If our snapshot of what was hot on Speedrun in Mar 2019 is anything to go by, then Link's a very busy boy indeed. As many as five Zelda games were in the 50 most popular, with A Link to the Past (Nintendo, 1991) the most played.

TOP TIMES #2

Ori and the Blind Forest: Definitive Edition

The *Definitive Edition* was similar to the director's cut of a movie. It added new areas to explore and a new "Dash" ability that granted Ori a burst of speed. As a result, this version is popular with speed-runners.

GAME	RUN TYPE	PLAYER	TIME	PLATFORM
New Super Mario Bros. 2	Any%	J_duude (CAN)	00:26:08	New 3DS
Octopath Traveler	Single Story; Ophilia	eLmaGus (DEU)	00:52:27	Switch
Ori and the Blind Forest: Definitive Edition	All Skills; No OOB/TA	Lucidus (USA)	00:27:43	PC
Portal	Out of Bounds	CantEven (USA)	00:07:07.920	PC
Refunct	Any%; Normal	xzRockin (USA)	00:02:43.830	PC
Resident Evil 2 (2019)	New Game (PC); Leon; Standard; 120	Orchlon (MNG)	00:53:02	PC
Resident Evil 5	New Game+ Solo; PC; Amateur	RuuDela (BRA)	01:21:53	PC
ROBLOX: Speed Run 4	No Skips; 5 Levels	kriptopolis (USA)	00:01:57.867	PC
The Simpsons: Hit & Run	All Story Missions; PC	LiquidWiFi (AUS)	01:26:23	PC
Slime Rancher	Any% Glitchless; 1.0.1 - 1.3.2	ThePigKing (UK)	00:14:26.45	PC
Splatoon 2	Hero Mode; Any%	hashedrice (JPN)	01:32:31	Switch
SpongeBob SquarePants: Battle for Bikini Bottom	No SBA	SHiFT (USA)	00:53:25	Xbox

RACC-CITY
J2198

Resident Evil 2 (2019)

Since its early-2019 release, Capcom's *Resident Evil* remake has taken Speedrun by storm. That's hardly a surprise, though, because, as with the original *RE2* from 1998, the game has modes of play that are dedicated to speed-running.

Super Mario Odyssey

Just like *The Legend of Zelda*, the top times in Super Mario's games are constantly being battled over. *Super Mario Odyssey* is the hottest ticket just now, with gamers still finding new tricks and shorter routes to knock vital seconds off their times.

GAME	RUN TYPE	PLAYER	TIME	PLATFORM
Spyro Reignited Trilogy	Spyro the Dragon; Any%	LuluPatate (USA)	00:27:25	PS4
Super Mario 64	120 Star; N64	cheese (ESP)	01:39:19	N64
Super Mario Bros.	Any%	somewes (USA)	00:04:55.796	NES
Super Mario Bros. 3	100%	mitchflowerpower (USA)	01:10:14	NES
Super Mario Odyssey	Any%; 1.0-1.1; 1P	Chaospringle (USA)	00:59:58	Switch
Super Mario Sunshine	Any%; Normal	nindiddeh (USA)	01:14:40	Wii
Super Mario World	96 Exit	Lui (ITA)	01:22:12.393	SNES
Super Metroid	Any%	Behemoth87 (UK)	00:40:56	SNES
Super Smash Bros. Melee	All Events	Fuzzyness (UK)	00:23:12.8	GameCube
Super Smash Bros. Ultimate	World of Light; NG+ Any%; Easy	haound (JPN)	02:25:21	Switch
Test Drive Unlimited	Tour of the Island	Ewil (CZE)	01:07:57	PC
Touhou Luna Nights	Any%	Remlerelyk (USA)	00:15:20	PC
Wii Sports Resort	All Sports	Alaskaxp2 (USA)	00:16:48	Wii U
Zero Deaths	Full Game; Current Patch	Akaya (DEU)	00:06:53.707	PC

Super Metroid

Just to prove that Nintendo's games are for life, Samus Aran's 1994 adventure for the SNES is another of the company's classic games that speed-runners can't stop playing.

SPORTING SUPERSTARS

Ever wanted to play world-class soccer like Ronaldo or jump into the ring as your favourite WWE star? Videogames let you do exactly that – and more. Here's our round-up of the greatest gaming sports stars of the past, present and future.

DANA BROOKE

Sport: WWE

Game: *WWE 2K19* (2K, 2018)

Born: 29 Nov 1988

Country: USA

Team: N/A

Dana Brooke has been a feisty presence in WWE since 2014 and now has three appearances in 2K's series under her belt. Playing as the glamorous wrestler, the UK's "TheGamerofGreat" recorded the **fastest completion of the Steel Cage 1v1 challenge in *WWE 2K19***. The PS4 player took just 45 sec to escape the cage, as verified by Speedrun on 9 Jan 2019.

ANTONIO BROWN

Sport: American football

Game: *Madden NFL 19* (EA, 2018)

Born: 10 Jul 1988

Country: USA

Team: Oakland Raiders

In real life, the wide receiver holds the record for the **most consecutive seasons for an NFL player to make 100 receptions** (six). He's also the cover star of *Madden NFL 19*. EA's gridiron franchise is the **longest-running sports videogame series**. From *John Madden Football*, released on 1 Jun 1988, to *Madden NFL 19* (10 Aug 2018), the series has run for 30 years 70 days.

AMANDA NUNES

Sport: UFC

Game: *UFC 3* (EA, 2018)

Born: 30 May 1988

Country: Brazil

Team: N/A

Nunes's defeat of Cris Cyborg on 29 Dec 2018 made her the **first female UFC fighter to hold two titles simultaneously**. The fight was even recreated in *UFC 3*, so players could re-live it. EA paid further homage to her success by making her the **highest-rated women's bantamweight division fighter in *UFC 3***. Her stats are: Striking 93, Grappling 89, Stamina 89 and Health 93 – a total of 364 out of 400.

BRYCE HARPER

Sport: Baseball

Game: *MLB The Show 19* (Sony, 2019)

Born: 16 Oct 1992

Country: USA

Team: Philadelphia Phillies

Sony's *MLB The Show* is the **best-selling PS4-exclusive sports series**, shifting 4.91 million copies as of 5 Feb 2019. Bryce Harper, the cover star of *MLB The Show 19*, held the **largest MLB contract for a baseball player** from 28 Feb 2019 to 20 Mar 2019. But his $330-m (£248.3-m) contract was topped when Mike Trout agreed a deal with the Los Angeles Angels worth $426.5 m (£321.3 m)!

CRISTIANO RONALDO

Sport: Soccer

Game: *FIFA 19* (EA, 2018)

Born: 5 Feb 1985

Country: Portugal

Team: Juventus

It was a close call, but *FIFA 19* cover star Ronaldo is also its **highest-rated player**. Ronaldo and perennial rival Lionel Messi both have overall ratings of 94, but the Portuguese edges out the Argentine on individual scores by 12 points – 468 to 456. The kit Ronaldo wears on the *FIFA 19* cover had to be retouched at the last minute to reflect his transfer from Real Madrid to Italian giants Juventus on 10 Jul 2018.

VINÍCIUS JÚNIOR

Sport: Soccer

Game: *FIFA 19* (EA, 2018)

Born: 12 Jul 2000

Country: Brazil

Team: Real Madrid

Some believe that Vinícius Júnior could well be one of the superstar players of the future. He's already making a name for himself as an attacker at Ronaldo's old club, Real Madrid, EA has recognized his potential in *FIFA 19*, where he is the youngest player to **make *FIFA 19*'s Ultimate Team Future Stars** – a squad of 21 outstanding young players that was announced on 25 Jan 2019.

GHEORGHE MUREȘAN

Sport: Basketball

Game: *NBA 2K19* (2K, 2018)

Born: 14 Feb 1971

Country: Romania

Team: All Time Washington Wizards

Basketball players are expected to be tall, but Gheorghe Mureșan is huge. He stands 231 cm (7 ft 7 in) – the **tallest player in NBA history**. It follows that he's also the **tallest player in *NBA 2K19***. But even he would have had to look up to Libya's Suleiman Ali Nashnush, who played in the 1960s. At an amazing 245 cm (8 ft 0.45 in) tall, he was the **tallest basketball player** ever.

WAYNE GRETZKY

Sport: Ice hockey

Game: *NHL 19* (EA, 2018)

Born: 26 Jan 1961

Country: Canada

Team: Edmonton Oilers

Where to start with this ice hockey icon? Of all the records he set on the rink, Gretzky's 2,857 points – the **most points scored in a National Hockey League career** – is a standout. His fame led to 10 games being named after him – the **most ice hockey videogames named after a player**. The first was *Wayne Gretzky Hockey* by THQ. It was released for the Amiga way back in 1988.

SUPERHEROES

In this chapter, you'll meet the heroes who strive to save the world from descending into chaos. But not before we introduce you to some of the villains who are causing it in the first place!

Most playable DC Comics characters in a game

In *LEGO® DC Super-Villains*, players can take a walk in the bad guy's shoes. Published by Warner Bros. on 16 Oct 2018, the game lets players assume control of all kinds of DC villains, from the well-known (The Joker, Harley Quinn, Lex Luthor and Darkseid) to those previously confined to comics of the past – The Ventriloquist, Mister Miracle and Virman Vundabar, anybody?

As confirmed to us by the game's publisher, the roster of playable villains (and heroes) amounts to 223, with 162 of those being available in the main game and the other 61 in paid-for DLC. Exhaust those and you can still create a brand-new villain, complete with your choice of evil powers.

COMING UP ▶▶▶

SPIDER-MAN

With his cool costume, super-strength and amazing agility, Spider-Man is the superhero that has it all – including a witty putdown for New York's villains. It's time to pull on your mask and get web-slinging!

NEMESIS ☠

There are plenty of villains out to give Spider-Man a very bad day, but it's the Green Goblin who causes Spidey the biggest headache. The Halloween-themed villain even starred in Spidey's first videogame (see bottom right).

THE AMAZING SPIDER-MAN

WOW!

3 HR 39 MIN 59 SEC

Sling-shotting his way to a blistering completion time of 3 hr 39 min 59 sec, "Kevbot43" (USA) achieved the fastest completion of *Marvel's Spider-Man* (Sony) on 11 Nov 2018. As verified by Speedrun, his time marks the first occasion that anyone has got below 3 hr 40 min in their bid to (very quickly) save New York City.

Largest gathering of people dressed as Spider-Man

To mark the launch of *Marvel's Spider-Man* (2018) for the PS4, Marvel and Sony teamed up to host a veritable multiverse of Spideys. In all, 547 suited-and-masked wall-crawlers convened at Comic Con Stockholm in Sweden on 16 Sep 2018.

EVOLUTION

Spidey's depiction in his games has changed monumentally over the years, but no matter the artwork, he still "does whatever a spider can"!

Spider-Man
Atari 2600 (1982)

Spider-Man vs.
The Kingpin (1991)

Spider-Man and
Venom: Maximum
Carnage (1994)

Spider-Man
SNES (1995)

Spider-Man
PSOne (2000)

First videogame to feature Stan Lee

The passing of Stan Lee in 2018 sent shockwaves through the world of entertainment. His first videogame performance was as the narrator of *Spider-Man* (2000) for the PSOne, where he greeted "true believers".

LOVE STORY

LOVE-O-METER

Gwen Stacy and Felicia Hardy have both fallen for Peter Parker's charms in Spider-Man lore, but Mary Jane Watson is his true love. "MJ" most recently appeared in *Marvel's Spider-Man* (2018) for PS4 (left), but made her gaming debut in Sega's *Spider-Man vs. The Kingpin* (1991).

3.3 MILLION

Swinging on to the PS4 on 7 Sep 2018, *Marvel's Spider-Man* was the fastest-selling PS4-exclusive title. According to VGChartz, it sold 3.3 million copies in three days of sale, 200,000 more than *God of War* (2018).

MOST PROLIFIC VIDEOGAME SUPERHERO

With the release of *Marvel's Spider-Man* on 7 Sep 2018, Spidey had web-slung and wall-crawled his way into 38 videogames that bear his name. Debuting in *Spider-Man* (1982) for the Atari 2600 (see below), he's since appeared on all kinds of consoles and in a huge variety of games. His closest competition, in terms of heroic appearances, is Batman, who'd headlined 35 games.

Spider-Man 2 (2004)

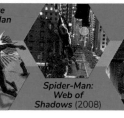

Ultimate Spider-Man (2005)

Spider-Man: Web of Shadows (2008)

Spider-Man: Edge of Time (2011)

The Amazing Spider-Man 2 (2014)

Marvel's Spider-Man (2018)

SNAPSHOT 📷

Spider-Man 2, the official game of the 2004 movie, was the **first Spider-Man game to offer true web-slinging**, where Spidey's webs actually attached to buildings and could be used to physically alter his trajectory. Before this, developers cheated by having his webs attach to the sky above him – now that really *would* be a super power!

First Marvel videogame

The Parker Brothers' vertical-scrolling *Spider-Man* game, released in 1982 for the Atari 2600, was the first official Marvel game. Players had to guide the wall-crawler to the top of a skyscraper and defuse a giant bomb, rescuing trapped residents and evading the Green Goblin while they were at it.

SUPERMAN

Is it a bird? Is it a plane? It's Superman! Or, depending on the Superman game you're playing, a collection of red and blue pixels that just about resemble a man. Despite being the **first superhero with superpowers**, his games – so far – haven't been particularly super.

Lowest-rated superhero videogame

Often known as *Superman 64*, *Superman: The New Superman Adventures* (Titus Software, 1999) was criticized for everything from its graphics to its gameplay. It's score of 22.9% on GameRankings is well and truly earned.

LOVE STORY

Lois Lane is an ace reporter for the *Daily Planet* and Clark Kent's better half. Depending on the game, comic book, TV show or film, Lois may or may not know that she's also dating Superman. But even she must get puzzled by the fact that he's always on hand to rescue her.

Best-selling game featuring Superman

We don't think the Man of Steel will be very happy to learn that the best-selling game to feature his super-self belongs to none other than the Dark Knight. *LEGO® Batman 2: DC Super Heroes* (2012) had sold 6.41 million units as of 14 Mar 2019, as verified by VGChartz.

NEMESIS

Since 1940, criminal mastermind Lex Luthor has hardly stopped hatching plans to get rid of Metropolis's meddlesome do-gooder. Frustration at his failed attempts could have Lex pulling his hair out – if he had any, that is!

Most game performances as Superman

Voice actor Travis Willingham has lent his vocal talents to the Man of Steel in four games (all published by Warner Bros.) – *LEGO Batman 2: DC Super Heroes*, *LEGO Batman 3: Beyond Gotham* (2014), *LEGO Dimensions* (2015) and *LEGO DC Super-Villains* (2018). He also voiced Mecha Superman in *Infinite Crisis* (Warner Bros., 2015).

First videogame with multiple screens

Until Atari's *Superman* came along in 1978, games were confined to a single screen – think *PAC-Man* or *Donkey Kong*. But in Atari's game, Superman could move to different screens to explore Metropolis. In the game, he had to thwart the evil plans of Lex Luthor – who else?

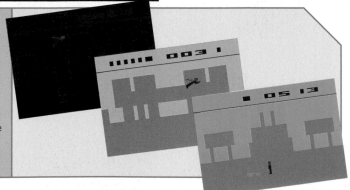

POWER-UP

Superman is known as the Man of Steel for a good reason (he's bulletproof), but he has other abilities that are just as useful...

Super-strength

Flight

Super-speed

Heat vision

Ice breath

Bulletproof

X-ray vision

FIRST FIRST-PARTY SUPERHERO GAME
Traditionally, most publishers license the super-powered stars of their games from the companies that own them – usually Marvel or DC. But this didn't apply to Superman's first videogame. When *Superman* was published for the Atari 2600 in Dec 1978, DC Comics held the rights to the character and Atari published the game. However, both companies were owned by Warner Communications, meaning the game was actually a first-party title.

Most cancelled superhero games
Like our hero laid low by kryptonite, five potential Superman games have sunk without trace. They were: a 1983 tie-in to the movie *Superman III* for the Atari 5200; a 1992 title from Sunsoft for the NES; a 1997 game from Neon Studios for the Game Boy; a 2000 game by Titus Software for the PlayStation; and "Blue Steel", a 2008 game for the PS3 by developer Factor 5 (above).

BATMAN

When a crime occurs in Gotham, you know that Batman will be on the case. The world's greatest detective uses his brains, as well as his brawn, to thwart some of the most unhinged super-villains ever to appear in games, comics, movies and beyond...

4,042 HITS

Batman: Arkham City (2011) put entire gangs of hoodlums in Batman's way, but skilled players were able to take them out in a series of linked punches and kicks. On 2 Jul 2015, "African Gamer" (NLD) produced the game's **longest combo**, registering 4,042 consecutive hits in the Iceberg Lounge VIP Room. The impressive combo lasted for over an hour.

First virtual-reality superhero videogame

Batman: Arkham VR (Warner Bros.) was the first superhero title to make use of VR technology. Released for the PS VR on 11 Oct 2016, it gave players the experience of first getting into Batman's suit and then using his many famous gadgets to solve the mystery of Nightwing's murder.

NEXT APPEARANCE

Batman hasn't had a game to call his own since 2016's *Arkham VR*, but rumours abound that he might be about to reach for the cowl once more. A Justice League team-up is hotly tipped, so we could see Superman and friends as well.

Most Batmobiles in a videogame

In the 2013 arcade-only racer *Batman* (Specular Interactive), the Caped Crusader can select from nine Batmobiles (below) for racing around Gotham. Each was inspired by the design of Batman's car from past TV shows, movies and games.

First videogame to guest star Batman

Batman had an unexpected appearance in Sega's *The Revenge of Shinobi* (1989) as a villain. As Sega failed to secure the rights to use the character, he was removed from later re-releases and replaced by a Devil-like creature.

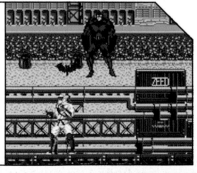

WEAPON SELECT

Batman's utility belt has a gadget for every occasion. Here's but a small sample of his wonderful toys.

Batarangs

Batclaw

Explosive Gel

Smoke Pellets

Line Launcher

Remote Hacking Device

Remote Electrical Charge Gun

MOST CRITICALLY ACCLAIMED SUPERHERO VIDEOGAME SERIES

For a long time, game developers struggled to capture Batman's tortured soul, but in 2009 developer Rocksteady finally cracked the conundrum with *Arkham Asylum*. Since then, three sequels have followed: *Arkham City* (2011), *Arkham Origins* (2013) and *Arkham Knight* (2015). With an average rating of 87.04% on GameRankings as of 1 Apr 2019, the *Arkham* series is the top-scoring superhero franchise.

NEMESIS ☠

There's nothing funny about having The Joker out to get you. The Clown Prince of Crime is about as insane as villains come, but Batman is usually able to stay one step ahead to beat him to the punchline.

WOLVERINE

With metal-covered claws, a fiery temperament and a decidedly unorthodox way of doing the right thing, Wolverine has won himself plenty of fans. But those that know him also know that Logan has a softer side.

First Nintendo Switch-exclusive superhero game

Nintendo struck a deal with Disney to publish *Marvel Ultimate Alliance 3: The Black Order*, with the Switch exclusive promised for late 2019. Wolverine was one of the familiar faces included in the game's trailer, and he'll be joined by the Avengers, as well as a host of other Marvel superheroes.

Disappearing act

On 1 Jan 2014, Activision withdrew eight superhero titles from digital distribution – the **most superhero games removed by a publisher from a streaming service at one time**. Five of them featured Wolverine. They were: *X-Men: The Official Game* (2006), *X-Men Origins: Wolverine* (2009), *X-Men: Destiny* (2011), *Spider-Man: Web of Shadows* (2008) and *Deadpool* (2013). The move came as a result of Activision losing the licensing rights to Marvel properties.

Most videogame voice credits as Wolverine

Steve Blum (USA) has voiced Logan in 18 games, beginning with *X-Men Legends* (2004). Despite playing Wolverine in nine movies, Hugh Jackman has voiced the mutant in just two games.

First arcade cabinet to support six players

Konami's 1992 *X-Men* arcade game encouraged team spirit with a colossal cabinet that could let up to six people play at once. To fit this many gamers into the same playing area, the cabinet doubled the available screen space by using two monitors.

LOVE STORY

Beneath his gruff exterior, Wolverine can be a sensitive soul. An initial spark of attraction between him and Jean Grey turned into a blazing fire of passion. But he seems destined to miss out on the love of his life, especially given she's committed to one of their fellow X-Men, Cyclops.

162

SUPPORTING CAST

Konami's landmark *X-Men* arcade cabinet (see below) had a stellar cast of super-powered mutants. Here are the good guys (not including Wolverine) that took on the maniacal Magneto.

Cyclops

Leader of the X-Men – blasts concussive beams from his eyes.

Colossus

Converts his body tissue into a super-durable exterior.

Storm

Harnesses the power of the weather to strike her enemies.

Nightcrawler

Teleporting, wall-scaling gymnast who's impossible to pin down.

Dazzler

Turns vibrations into laser beams to confuse enemies.

FIRST GAME TO STAR WOLVERINE AS THE LEAD CHARACTER

Wolverine's first outing as the protagonist of a game came in 1991's *Wolverine* (below). Produced by the now-defunct developer Software Creations, the NES title was a side-scrolling platformer that pitted the fierce X-Man against Sabretooth and Magneto.

Logan made his debut as a supporting character even earlier – in 1989. *The Uncanny X-Men* was released by LJN, again for the NES. The top-down adventure game saw Wolverine teaming up with Colossus, Cyclops, Storm, Nightcrawler and Iceman.

SCORE 003500   HAYOK
STRENGTH   AI

NEMESIS

He may share similar regenerative powers to Wolverine, but Sabretooth doesn't have any of Logan's heroic leanings. Despite working together at various points, the pair have developed a bitter and violent rivalry.

GOKU

Time and again in *Dragon Ball Z* showdowns, Goku is the underdog and seemingly outmatched. But the Super Saiyan always rises to the challenge thanks to his iron will, the ability to raise his power level and, of course, his "Kamehameha"!

Most critically acclaimed *Dragon Ball* game

Goku looks more than happy with the news that *Dragon Ball FighterZ* (Bandai Namco, 2018) is the best-received game to be based on *Dragon Ball*. As of 8 Mar 2018, the PS4 version had an average score of 86.76% at GameRankings, across 36 reviews. The title was praised for its balanced gameplay and a visual style that's extremely faithful to *Dragon Ball Z* – the television show on which it's based.

$28,497

Dragon Ball FighterZ (*DBFZ*) pro gamer "SonicFox" (aka Dominique McLean, USA) had picked up $28,497 (£22,092) as of 12 Feb 2019 – the **most money earned playing *DBFZ***. McLean has won numerous events since the game's 2018 release, including EVO 2018 (USA), VSFighting 2018 (UK) and DreamHack Austin 2018 (USA).

NEMESIS

Frieza and his army of super-powered aliens very nearly reduced the galaxy to ashes. Even Goku could barely defy the tyrant, until he was pushed so far that the true power of the Super Saiyan awoke within him.

First manga character in Macy's Thanksgiving Day Parade

At just over 21.3 m (70 ft) long, Goku had a very *inflated* opinion of himself at the Macy's Day Parade. On 22 Nov 2018, the Saiyan floated through the streets of New York City, USA, as part of the city's famous annual parade. The balloon representation of the Japanese comic-book star required 90 handlers to guide it.

257,805 VIEWERS

More than a quarter of a million people tuned in to Twitch on 5 Aug 2018 to watch the *Dragon Ball FighterZ* EVO 2018 main event take place in Las Vegas, Nevada, USA – the **most concurrent viewers for an EVO Twitch event**. The eventual winner of the tournament was "SonicFox" (see above right), who took home $15,474 (£11,896) in winnings.

SUPPORTING CAST

When Frieza, Cell or any other bad guy comes calling, Goku's allies are there by his side, ready to help out wherever they can.

Kuririn

Goku's oldest friend and cheerleader.

Yamcha

Always there to help, no matter the odds.

Piccolo

Former rival, but now trusted friend.

Vegeta

Will fight anyone to prove his power.

Bulma

Genius scientist and wife of Vegeta.

Gohan

Goku's son is a chip off the old block.

MOST PROLIFIC MANGA-BASED VIDEOGAME CHARACTER

Before he made an appearance in a game, or even in the *Dragon Ball Z* TV show, a young Goku was the lead character of the *Dragon Ball* manga. The comic was a regular feature in Japan's *Weekly Shōnen Jump* magazine, with Goku debuting in 1984. Since then, his fame – like his strength – has grown and grown, and the Super Saiyan has since starred in 80 games. His first gaming appearance was in Epoch's *Dragon Ball: Dragon Daihikyō*, released for the Super Cassette Vision console (a mostly Japan-only system) in 1986. The most recent title was Bandai Namco's *Jump Force* on 15 Feb 2019 – a game named after the magazine in which he first appeared.

Fastest 100% completion of *Dragon Ball FighterZ* (Arcade)

American gamer "Xur" took 56 min 36 sec to clear the "Arcade" mode of *Dragon Ball FighterZ*, as verified by Speedrun on 27 Jun 2018. The speed-runner used the formidable trio of Vegito (left), Android 16 (middle) and Beerus (right). No Goku in sight, you might think. But anyone who knows their *Dragon Ball* well is aware that Vegito is a fusion of Goku and Vegeta.

LOVE STORY

LOVE-O-METER

Chi-Chi is Goku's wife and the mother of their children, Gohan and Goten. She might be *only* human, but her fiery temper and love for her family keeps Goku and their super-strong offspring in check. She's even a playable character in a few games, most notably in Bandai Namco's *Super Dragon Ball Z* (2005).

BAYONETTA

With magical hair and pistols in her high heels, Bayonetta took the hack-and-slash genre to an entirely different level when she made her entrance in 2009. The Umbra Witch has continued to mix style and substance ever since.

NEXT APPEARANCE

Bayonetta 3 was announced in Dec 2017, but details have been scant since then. We know it will be a Switch exclusive and that the series' developer, PlatinumGames, will lead on design. That alone should mean it's worth waiting for.

Most used *Super Smash Bros. for Wii U* character at EVO 2018

At EVO 2018 in Las Vegas, Nevada, USA, three of the four finalists in the *Super Smash Bros. for Wii U* event on 5 Aug chose to play as Bayonetta. She was a controversial selection, with many in the fighting-game community regarding her as overpowered. "Lima" (Bharat Chintapalli, USA) emerged victorious, but the fans weren't happy.

Highest Xbox 360 score in *Famitsu*

Regarded as the definitive source of review scores in Japan, weekly magazine *Famitsu* gave the Xbox 360 version of *Bayonetta* a perfect 40/40 score. In its history, *Famitsu* has awarded just 25 games a perfect score and *Bayonetta* is the only Xbox-specific version on the list. The PS3 version scored a slightly lower 38/40, owing to some minor frame-rate issues.

WEAPON SELECT

The Umbra Witch has a host of magical moves at her disposal, but she can add to her armoury with a series of lethal extras. Each comes with its own range of special attacks, which can be interwoven to unleash ever-more-deadly combos.

Shuraba	Pillow Talk	Sai Fung
A good blade for the *Bayonetta* beginner.	*Star Wars*-inspired green-energy weapon.	Deadly mix of a gun and nunchucks.

NEMESIS ☠

Balder is a Lumen Sage who seeks to rule over the three realms of Paradiso, the Human World and Inferno. Only Bayonetta has the strength to stop him – and only those who reach the game's finale will find out why.

First in-game spoken articulation of Enochian

Bayonetta's angels and demons speak Enochian, a strange language that was supposedly revealed to real-life 16th-century occultist John Dee. *Dante's Inferno* (2010) and *ZombiU* (2012) used some elements, but *Bayonetta* was the first game with characters who spoke it.

MOST COMBO ATTACKS PERFORMED USING HAIR

Bayonetta's hair is more than just a fashion statement. She uses her flowing locks to clothe herself, and her hair is also her most potent weapon. With "Wicked Weaves", for example, Bayonetta can summon the gigantic fists and feet of Madama Butterfly – a demon that grants her power to Bayonetta. Other attacks called "Infernal Weaves" call forth demons, including Baal and Diomedes. Her hair is used in 56 combos in *Bayonetta* (Sega, 2009) and 62 in *Bayonetta 2* (Nintendo, 2014).

Scarborough Fair

Our heroine's go-to set of four guns.

Lt. Col. Kilgore

Rocket launcher with apocalyptic power.

Kulshedra

Whip infused with a serpent demon.

10 MILLION HALOS

The Rodin are golden rings that Bayonetta wears on her wrists and ankles. They're among the most damage-dealing weapons in the game, which is why they're the **most expensive weapon** at 10 million halos. But before you can wield them, you must confront and defeat Rodin himself (right).

1 HR 42 MIN 36 SEC

On 15 Oct 2018, Dutch gamer "AceKrana" raced through *Bayonetta* to achieve the game's **fastest completion**. The PC player's time was verified by Speedrun, but the gamer bemoaned "mess ups here and there". "AceKrana" is already eyeing up a faster time, saying that the 1-hr 41-min barrier is "getting closer".

OVERWATCH

Blizzard's hero-shooter crashed on to the scene in 2016, bringing with it a slew of heroes (not to mention a couple of villains). The game is now a seriously competitive e-sport, and there's even a dedicated *Overwatch* League (OWL) for fans to follow.

First female in the *Overwatch* League

When she joined the Shanghai Dragons in Feb 2018, "Geguri" (aka Kim Se-yeon, KOR) made history. The e-sports pro – who is known for playing as the Tank character Zarya (above) – joined the OWL team from the ROX Orcas (a pro team, but not an OWL franchise). "I thought this would help me improve as a player," she said.

Highlights from the *Overwatch* League Grand Finals

On 28 Jul 2018 at the Barclays Center in Brooklyn, New York City, USA, the London Spitfire were crowned the **first champions of the *Overwatch* League Grand Finals** (see pp.8–9 for more).

Three of the Spitfire's players hogged the headlines, with "Profit" (aka Park Joon-yeong, KOR – pictured below centre) in the spotlight. On the way to victory over the Philadelphia Fusion, "Profit" dealt 86,924 points of damage – the **most inflicted in the Grand Finals**. For his efforts, he was later named the **first *Overwatch* League Grand Finals MVP (most valuable player)**.

"Fury" (aka Kim Jun-ho, KOR – far left) emerged from battle with the **fewest deaths** against his name. He was eliminated just 23 times. The elusive pro also achieved the **most eliminations**, taking down the Fusion's players on 189 occasions.

Rather more benign was teammate "NUS" (aka Kim Jong-seok, KOR – pictured near left). Playing as healing-class character Mercy, he restored 108,436 points of damage to his London Spitfire colleagues – the **most healing in the Grand Finals** – as they marched to the OWL's Season 1 trophy.

WEAPON SELECT

Just as the *Overwatch* heroes all have their distinct personalities, so too do they have their signature armaments. Many gamers love the satisfaction of bashing enemies to bits with Reinhardt's Rocket Hammer, while others prefer the healing factor of Mercy's Caduceus Staff. Here are some of the most damage-dealing examples.

Hellfire Shotguns

Reaper's shotguns rip his enemies apart.

Particle Cannon

Zarya's cannon is lethal at short range.

LOVE STORY

Rumours about supposed *Overwatch* relationships abound, but there's no doubt that Tracer and Emily are an item. Blizzard confirmed in Dec 2016 that Tracer is the game's **first LGBT character**. Her partner was first seen in a digital comic, *Reflections* – she's seen here giving Tracer a kiss.

42 MATCHES

The Shanghai Dragons are the not-so-proud owners of the record for the **longest losing streak for an e-sports team**. The team lost all 40 games of the 2018 OWL season and the first two of the 2019 season as well. Their barren run came to an end on 22 Feb 2019, when they beat the Boston Uprising 3–1.

MOST REGISTERED PLAYERS FOR A PAID-FOR HERO-SHOOTER

While the free-to-play online shooter *Fortnite* has dominated the realms of the battle royale, *Overwatch* has earned itself a notable record in the arena of the paid-for hero-shooter. As of May 2018, 40 million gamers had signed up, according to information released by Blizzard. In the seven months from Oct 2017 to May 2018, *Overwatch* added five million players. When it comes to **most registered players for a free-to-play hero-shooter**, it's EA's *Apex Legends* in front (see pp.106–07).

The Viper

Where Ashe goes, her semi-automatic goes too.

Endothermic Blaster

Helps Mei put enemies into deep freeze.

Rocket Hammer

Reinhardt's iconic melee weapon.

Peacekeeper

McCree's six-shooter does heavy damage.

$90 MILLION

The **largest e-sports streaming deal** was struck on 9 Jan 2018. Online streaming platform Twitch paid at least $90 m (£66.37 m) to *Overwatch* developer and publisher Blizzard to buy exclusive streaming rights for two years of the OWL. Coverage is streamed globally (except in China) in Korean, English and French.

Most played hero in *Competitive Overwatch*

As of Season 13 of Competitive Play (which started on 1 Nov 2018), Reinhardt is the most selected character. Across the seven ranks, he came out on top in the Bronze, Silver, Gold and Platinum categories, and second for Diamond, Master and Grandmaster. He was beaten in those categories by Ana.

Here there be Monsters

Clubbed tail can knock even monster-hunters off their feet

Watch out for fireballs

Rathalos

A Rathalos is a formidable foe in any *Monster Hunter* game. But the mighty wyvern is a record holder thanks to its appearance in *Super Smash Bros. Ultimate* (2018), where it became the **first character to appear as a boss and an assist trophy** in Nintendo's latest brawler.

Videogames have a habit of pitting you against all manner of ferocious beasts and nightmare creatures. Enjoy our pictorial guide to the gaming world's most savage monsters.

Headcrab

Valve forum user "Darkside55" was so inspired by *Half-Life*'s facehugging critters that he wrote a book about them. *Everything you wanted to know about Headcrabs… and more* – all 28,000 words of it – was published online in 2006.

fangs contain zombifying mutagens

Distinctive horns to terrify victims

Cleric Beast

The "Cleric Beast" trophy, earned when players defeat *Bloodborne*'s first boss, is the **most common *Bloodborne* trophy**. Despite this, only 48.9% of those who own Sony's 2015 hit have unlocked it, according to PSNProfiles. This means that the horror has shown the door to more than half of those who have faced it!

Deadly claws to tear its prey apart

Bioluminescent chemicals turn red when agitated

Beware! Drill used for more than just digging

GUINNESS WORLD RECORDS

Big Daddy

Big Daddies in *BioShock* (2K Games, 2007) usually have only one hand, with the other replaced by a socking great drill. In the 2010 sequel, you even play as one of these lumbering bio-weapons. So, for maximum authenticity, "BloodThunder" (USA) charged through its campaign using just one hand. The **fastest one-handed completion of *BioShock 2*** took 1 hr 53 min 51 sec on 6 Jul 2014, as verified by Speedrun.

George

George, the gorilla in Midway's 1986 arcade game *Rampage*, also stars in the **highest-grossing movie based on a videogame** – and alongside Dwayne Johnson, no less! At the worldwide box office as of 15 Mar 2019, Warner Bros.' *Rampage* (2018) had taken $428,056,280 (£322,865,000), as verified by The Numbers.

Toughened skull for charging attacks

Armour plating hides weak spot

Cenobia

Speed-runners of *Shadow of the Colossus* (Sony, 2018) compete over the "Boss Rush" run, where they seek to quickly topple the game's 16 beasts. On 14 Jan 2019, "ChurchNEOH" (USA) recorded the **fastest completion of the "Boss Rush" challenge** in 34 min 32 sec. Of all the colossi felled, the bull-like Cenobia put up the most resistance.

Big biceps for levelling buildings

Monokuma

Monokuma, the fearsome headmaster of Hope's Peak Academy, couldn't pass up the chance to become the **first teddy bear to physically appear on a PS4 console**. The Japan-exclusive, limited-edition console was released to celebrate the launch of *Danganronpa V3: Killing Harmony* on 12 Jan 2017.

Don't trust his two-faced grin!

CARTOON ICONS

Videogames and cartoon visuals go together like Mario and Peach. Here, we take a look at some of the characters whose games look like they should be on Saturday-morning TV.

Fastest-selling Nintendo game

Mario, Luigi, Pikachu, Samus, Link and the other stars of the Nintendo neighbourhood are famous enough in their own right. But bring them together, then sprinkle in some famous faces from other franchises, and you have something truly incredible. On 31 Dec 2018, Nintendo revealed that *Super Smash Bros. Ultimate* for the Switch was its fastest-selling game of all time. After its release on 7 Dec 2018, the cartoon brawler sold 12.08 million copies in just 24 days. By comparison, Nintendo's previous fastest-seller was *New Super Mario Bros. Wii* (2009), which shifted 1.4 million in a week.

COMING UP ▶▶▶▶

MICKEY MOUSE

For someone who is approaching his 100th birthday, Mickey Mouse is wearing remarkably well. Indeed, you could say he's looking better than ever. The world's most famous rodent brings fun anywhere he treads... and that includes his games.

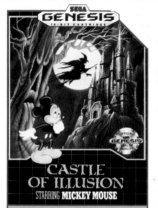

Mickey – meet Oswald

Before Mickey came along, Disney was busy creating cartoons that starred Oswald the Lucky Rabbit. However, a disagreement back in 1928 led to Disney losing the rights to Oswald, hence the arrival of Mickey. Disney would finally unite the pair in 2010's *Epic Mickey* – the **first game starring Oswald the Lucky Rabbit and Mickey Mouse.**

21 MIN 6 SEC

On 28 Dec 2017, Australia's "mr_double07" took 21 min 6 sec to set the **fastest completion of** *Castle of Illusion Starring Mickey Mouse* **on "Hard" difficulty.** Published by Sega in 1990, the classic Genesis (Mega Drive) platformer remains one of Mickey's most-loved outings to this day and still entices speed-runners.

$250

The **most valuable Mickey Mouse videogame** is a Mickey-branded Nintendo Game & Watch, released on 9 Oct 1981. Used copies of the game cost $250 (£188) on average, according to data provided by PriceCharting on 3 Dec 2018. In the game, Mickey has to catch eggs in a basket as they roll towards him from four different chicken coops.

EVOLUTION

Like all classic gaming characters, Mickey Mouse's appearance has improved as home consoles have become more powerful. No matter the technology, though, getting Mickey's famous ears right has always been the key to making him look the part.

LOVE STORY

Minnie is the other half of what must be the world's most famous animated couple. Though their wedding has never been committed to film, they're married. It means that in the *Kingdom Hearts* games, Minnie enjoys the lofty status of Queen of Disney Castle.

First Mickey Mouse toy inspired by a toys-to-life videogame

The *Disney Infinity* toys-to-life series is no longer being produced, but it did leave plenty of new toys as its legacy. Among these were the Mickey Mouse and Pluto Toybox action figures, released in Aug 2018. So that their owners could match the poses of the characters from the game, the figures were made to be very adaptable. For example, Mickey's arms can bend at 14 points!

BEST-SELLING VIDEOGAME STARRING MICKEY MOUSE

In the *Kingdom Hearts* series, Mickey Mouse is known as King Mickey, the monarch of Disney Castle. In terms of sales, Square Enix's RPGs certainly rule over all other games to feature the Disney icon. First released in 2002, the original *Kingdom Hearts* for the PS2 has sold 6.4 million units, making it the best-selling game to feature Mickey (however briefly). But that baton looks set to pass to *Kingdom Hearts III* (2019). The latest in the series sold 5 million units in its first week (see p.38), though sales reports have gone quiet since.

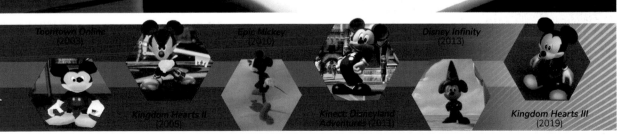

Toontown Online (2003)

Kingdom Hearts II (2005)

Epic Mickey (2010)

Kinect: Disneyland Adventures (2011)

Disney Infinity (2013)

Kingdom Hearts III (2019)

Most substitutes for Mickey Mouse in one game

A quirk of copyright law meant that one game became three in 1993. Kemco's *Mickey Mouse IV: Mahō no Labyrinth* (top left) starred Mickey Mouse in Japan. But in the US the same game became *The Real Ghostbusters* (above centre), and then in Europe it became *Garfield Labyrinth* (top right).

NEMESIS ☠

Pete has been pestering Mickey since as far back as 1928, when Disney decided that its leading mouse needed an antagonist in the shape of a cat. He was up to his old tricks yet again in Square Enix's *Kingdom Hearts III* (2019).

SPYRO THE DRAGON

With his fiery temperament and heroic nature, Spyro is one of gaming's most popular characters. Part of his charm is that he has a mischievous side, but it's this that can often land him in hot water with his friends.

NEMESIS ☠

Even by the standards of the bad guys you have met so far, it's hard to find anything nice to say about Gnasty Gnorc – he's mean, rude, always angry and he even hates dragons. Good job we have Spyro on our side.

Rarest Skylanders figure

To promote *Skylanders: Spyro's Adventure* at E3 2011, Activision created 600 specially marked figures. Lucky media recipients were offered a Spyro, Gill Grunt or Trigger Happy figure. They came in a rare package with an invite to "bring me to life at the Activision E3 booth". The figures are now highly collectable.

First Spyro mobile videogame

Spyro's debut on mobile devices arrived before Android and iPhone smartphones had even been invented. *Spyro* (Vivendi) was an isometric adventure released in Jun 2003. In the game, Spyro had to help fairies find outfits to wear to a ball.

SUPPORTING CAST

Spyro's animal allies are a source of support, with most having recurring roles across the series. Here, we profile the characters who help Spyro out most often.

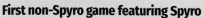

Hunter
Loyalty is his middle name, but he can be duped by the devious out there.

Sheila
Calm and easy-going – until you rattle her cage.

Moneybags
Loves money and refuses to do something for nothing.

First non-Spyro game featuring Spyro

The teams behind Crash Bandicoot and Spyro mixed socially, so it made sense that their creations should also interact. Spyro didn't make the starting grid of 1999's *Crash Team Racing*, but the purple dragon got behind the wheel in its sequel, *Crash Nitro Kart* (2003) – though only on the Game Boy Advance version of the popular racer.

Rarest *Spyro* trophy

The "Call Me Fireman!" trophy in *Skylanders: Spyro's Adventure* (2011) is the hardest non-Platinum trophy to acquire in any game to star Spyro. As of 25 Feb 2019, only 1.6% of PS3 players had earned the trophy, unlocked by beating Kaos's minions in the Lava Lakes Railway level with just Gill Grunt's Power Hose.

FASTEST COMPLETION OF THE
SPYRO REIGNITED TRILOGY

In 2018, the original three *Spyro* games were given a new lease of life. The *Spyro Reignited Trilogy* (Activision) updated Spyro's classic adventures with improved graphics and all-new voice acting. But what speed-runners really cared about was getting their teeth into yet more *Spyro* platforming! On 7 Dec 2018, "Jumpyluff" (USA) completed the so-called "Trifecta" run of all three games in 1 hr 32 min 56 sec on PS4, a time that was verified by Speedrun.

Bianca
Possesses supernatural powers, but the spells don't always turn out well.

Sparx the Dragonfly
Never leaves Spyro's side for a second. Has saved his friend many times.

Agent 9
Always ready with a laser blaster and an itchy trigger finger.

LOVE STORY

Cynder has turned her life around after starting out as one of Spyro's most dangerous enemies. By doing what he does best, Spyro was able to free her from the corrupting influence of the evil dragon Malefor. Ever since then, she's had the hots for him.

90.59%

The *Spyro* series proved a hit with fans from the off, but it was with *Spyro: Year of the Dragon* (Sony, 2000) that the franchise took wing. As the **most critically acclaimed *Spyro* title**, it has a collective score of 90.59% from 23 reviews, according to GameRankings. One review commented on "outstanding visuals" in "Spyro's best outing to date".

177

RAYMAN

Ubisoft's platforming hero has never let a little thing like the lack of a limb (or four) dampen his spirits. Rayman pulls no punches when it comes to saving the day – and he's not opposed to getting down to a phat beat when the opportunity arises, either.

BOSS FIGHT

The roster of bewildering bad guys you must face in Rayman's 1995 debut includes a malevolent saxophone and a rolling-pin-wielding spacewoman. Just a normal day at the office, then...

Bzzit

Moskito

Mr Sax

Mr Stone

Space Mama

Mr Skops

Mr Dark

NEMESIS

What else would any self-respecting villain do but look to steal the source of balance in the world? Mr Dark's theft of the all-powerful Great Pontoon plunges Rayman's world into chaos and sparks his first adventure.

Best-selling *Rayman* title
It took 18 years for the original *Rayman* (Ubisoft, 1995) on the PSOne to have its sales exceeded by another game in the series. *Rayman Legends* (2013) was the game to do so. As of 4 Feb 2019, it had sold 4.48 million physical copies across multiple platforms, according to VGChartz.

20 MIN 36 SEC
Invasions Sprints are special timed levels in 2013's *Rayman Legends*. They're tricky enough as it is, but speed-runners need absolute precision in their every movement to clock the fastest times. Impressively, on 10 Oct 2018, "Martini" took 20 min 36 sec to set the **fastest completion of all Invasions Sprint levels** on the PC version, as verified by Speedrun.

SNAPSHOT 📷

Mexican skeletons belting out a mariachi-style version of Survivor's hit "Eye of the Tiger" is just one of the highlights of *Rayman Legends'* joyful music levels.

Rarest PlayStation trophy in a *Rayman* game
An HD remaster of *Rayman 3* appeared on the PS3 in 2012, bringing with it trophies. Many say the game is tough to crack, and the 0.5% unlock rate (verified by PSNProfiles) of the "Perfection Needs No Arms" trophy seems to support that theory. It demands that players complete every level with a perfect score.

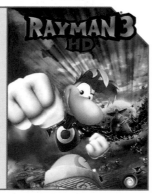

Most critically acclaimed *Rayman* game
Rayman 2: The Great Escape (2000) for the Sega Dreamcast has an approval rating of 93.05%, according to GameRankings. That also makes it the sixth-highest-rated Sega Dreamcast game.

RAREST *RAYMAN* VIDEOGAME

On 23 Oct 2016, Ubisoft game designer Michel Ancel took to Instagram to announce the rediscovery of a *Rayman* game for the Super NES, last worked on in 1992. The game was abandoned in favour of beginning production on *Rayman* (1995) for the PSOne. Ancel's comment alongside the image of the prototype cartridge read: "Incroyable !!!! We have found the old unique *Rayman* SNES ROM !!!! It was sleeping for 24 years ..... Time to wake it up !!!!" Only one copy of the game is thought to exist.

179

ŌKAMI AMATERASU

It's not every game that allows you to play as a sun goddess in the form of a white wolf. A critically acclaimed action-adventure whose sales never quite matched its plaudits, Capcom's *Ōkami* (2006) created a graceful gaming experience that delved deep into Japanese mythology.

Fastest time to earn the Top Dog trophy

Record holder and *Ōkami* fan "Kinnin11" strives for perfection. The Dutch gamer shaved even more time off his previous best on 1 Feb 2019. He claimed every trophy in 8 hr 39 min, as verified by Speedrun.

Issun

Listen, Ammy... Ever heard of the spirits of the brush?

First Kanji tutorial in a videogame

Japanese words – and specifically the pictogram style of writing called Kanji – are at the heart of *Ōkami*. Players must write characters in the script to use magic, so the game includes a Kanji-writing tutorial.

First game to have new box art mailed to customers

In 2008, North American fans of *Ōkami* were treated to an unexpected bonus after the release of Amaterasu's adventure for the Nintendo Wii. The original artwork sleeve contained a watermark from gaming website IGN, causing red faces at Capcom USA. As a result, Capcom designed three new sleeves that fans could either request by mail or download from the company's website.

SNAPSHOT

Part of *Ōkami*'s charm is the Celestial Brush. Players can use the PS2's analogue sticks to draw symbols on the screen. These alter the environment by building bridges or blowing up obstacles.

Longest soundtrack for an action-adventure game

With 217 songs and a running time of 5 hr 36 min, the soundtrack for *Ōkami* is spectacularly extensive for a single action-adventure, as well as quite beautiful. Harmonious rivals include *Metal Gear Solid V*, at 3 hr 3 min, and *Horizon Zero Dawn*, at just over 4 hr.

POWER-UP

As Ōkami travels throughout Japan, she learns new ways to use the Celestial Brush, unlocking an ever-expanding array of magical skills. Here is just a sample of the magical characters at her disposal.

Sunrise

Power Slash

Bloom

Cherry Bomb

Inferno

Galestorm

Rejuvenation

Fastest completion of *Ōkamiden*

In Capcom's 2010 sequel to *Ōkami* for the Nintendo DS, you play not as Amaterasu but as her son, Chibiterasu. The Netherlands' "Kinnin11" – of Top Dog trophy fame (see far left) – had the young pup bound through the adventure in 5 hr 13 min 19 sec, as verified by Speedrun on 5 Aug 2016.

NEMESIS

Yamata no Orochi is a villain straight out of Japanese folklore. The gigantic, eight-headed dragon was expelled from Takamagahara (Heaven) for tricking Amaterasu and has snacked on humans ever since...

MOST CRITICALLY ACCLAIMED GAME WITH AN ANIMAL HERO

The gorgeous art style and animation used to bring Capcom's magical white wolf to life helped make *Ōkami* for the PS2 the most critically acclaimed game of all time to feature an animal hero. As of 7 Feb 2019, the game had an aggregate score of 92.65% from 73 reviews, according to GameRankings. The nearest game with animal icons at its core is Nintendo's *Pokémon Silver* (1999) – its average score is 91.35%.

CONTRIBUTORS

MATT BRADFORD

Matt is a writer, editor and voice actor who's been gaming since his parents brought home an Intellivision. He can be heard on the *Video Game Outsiders*, *ZombieCast* and *NoSleep* podcasts.

Which games did you play most this year?
God of War, *Marvel's Spider-Man* (above), *Assassin's Creed Odyssey*, *Observer* and *Thronebreaker: The Witcher Tales*.

What was the year's most exciting gaming event?
Announcements about new consoles, the evolution of VR and the rise of streaming. Google Stadia is promising unprecedented accessibility and console-makers are touting true "next-gen" experiences. Whether they make good on the promises remains to be seen, but it bodes well we're seeing so much experimentation.

ROB CAVE

Rob is a veteran writer and editor on videogames, popular science and all things pop-cultural. He's worked on every *Gamer's Edition* since its launch, and still can't walk past a *Galaga* arcade cabinet without the urge to insert coins.

Which games did you play most this year?
This year, I've been mostly playing *Red Dead Redemption 2*, and *Apex Legends* (above) to keep my battle-royale multiplayer skills sharp.

What was the year's most exciting gaming event?
I think it's probably a tie between the launch of Google's Stadia and the announcement of Apple Arcade. Both are potentially massively disruptive to gaming as we know it.

THOMAS McCURDY

Thomas is the production coordinator at Guinness World Records. When he's not chasing editors with deadlines or clogging the printer, he's burying himself in a mixture of RPGs, *Souls* games and strangely bittersweet walking simulators.

Which games did you play most this year?
Hollow Knight (above), *Octopath Traveler* and *Oxenfree* – the Switch is genuinely a blessing if you've got a long commute, and the indie catalogue is phenomenal.

What was the year's most exciting gaming event?
The release of *Sekiro: Shadows Die Twice* and the news that *Hollow Knight: Silksong* is a full game, not just DLC. It's a good time for fans of wandering cautiously around ruined kingdoms!

JONATHAN PARKYN

Jonathan writes about games, technology and virtually anything else people will pay him for. Credits include writing TV shows for the BBC and Sky. His favourite console is his original 1983 ColecoVision, which still works (despite 36 years of button-mashing his way through *Zaxxon*).

Which games did you play most this year?
As a die-hard *Souls* fan, I've been mostly dying hard again and again in *Sekiro: Shadows Die Twice*. This year, I've also played way too much *Red Dead 2* (above), *Gris* and *Trials Rising*.

What was the year's most exciting gaming event?
Easy. *The Legend of Zelda: Link's Awakening* Switch remake reveal trailer!

PAUL DAVIES

Paul fell in love with videogames in 1978 and has been writing about them since 1992. He now works on many books about the making of the biggest hits. Between times, Paul enjoys being a creative consultant to the videogame industry and being trusted with awesome secrets.

Which games did you play most this year?
I've been revisiting many 8-bit and 16-bit favourites, including *Mega Man* and *Sonic the Hedgehog* (above). I blame my little boy, but it's been great.

What was the year's most exciting gaming event?
The invasion of heart and minds that is *Fortnite.* It's been an education for so many people, whether you like it or not.

STACE HARMAN

Co-founder and director of IndieByDesign.net, Stace is a writer, author and game-design consultant. He's been writing about games for 10 years and playing them for more than 30.

Which games did you play most this year?
Sekiro: Shadows Die Twice (above), in which I died several hundred times, *SteamWorld Quest: Hand of Gilgamech,* to scratch the strategy itch, and *Beat Saber,* to de-stress at the end of many a long week and record hilarious family videos.

What was the year's most exciting gaming event?
Getting a proper look at *The Last of Us Part II*, gearing up for the next generation of game technology and the *Sonic the Hedgehog* movie blowing minds across the globe.

JOHN ROBERTSON

IndieByDesign.net co-founder and director, John is a writer, consultant and author with over a decade's experience in the entertainment industry. He will beat you at battle-royale games.

Which games did you play most this year?
Apex Legends (above), *Fortnite, Divinity: Original Sin II, Yakuza Kiwami* and *Puyo Puyo Tetris.*

What was the year's most exciting gaming event?
The increase in the number of large videogame publishers seeking to understand and expand on the benefits, for themselves and players, of the free-to-play model. It allows for more exposure to more players of a range of different games that they might otherwise have not engaged with.

JACK TURNER

Jack is a tech journalist by day and freelance games writer by night, covering games for publications such as *The Independent.* He's also a regular on the *GWR Gamer's Podcast*.

Which games did you play most this year?
Hitman 2, Captain Toad: Treasure Tracker (above) and *Beat Saber.*

What was the year's most exciting gaming event?
Although it's early days, Google's Stadia platform could have a radical impact on the gaming industry. Being able to play a brand-new game instantly at the click of a button shows how far we've come. The reveal raised more questions than answers, but Stadia's definitely one to watch!

183

INDEX

INDEX

INDEX

PICTURE CREDITS

Cover Microsoft, Nintendo, Epic Games, Activision, Warner Bros., Matt Makes Games, Sega, Sony, Square Enix, EA; **1** Capcom, Sega, Activision, EA, Epic Games; **5** Epic Games, Nintendo, Microsoft; **8** Getty, Shutterstock; **10** Getty; **11** Terry Gates/NC State University; **16** Alamy, Shutterstock; **17** Alamy, Shutterstock; **20** Shinsuke Kamioka/GWR; **21** Alamy; **32** Jason Sussman; **34** Alamy; **35** Alamy, Getty; **44** Shutterstock; **54** Shutterstock; **55** Getty, Shutterstock; **70** Kevin Scott Ramos/GWR; **80** Shutterstock; **81** IMDB; **82** Getty, Andy Park; **83** Shutterstock; **98** Shutterstock; **102** Shutterstock; **118** Getty; **124** Shutterstock; **138** Shutterstock; **152** Shutterstock, Getty; **156** Alamy, Shutterstock; **157** Shutterstock; **158** Shutterstock; **160** Shutterstock; **162** Getty; **164** Getty; **168** Alamy, Shutterstock

ACKNOWLEDGEMENTS

Guinness World Records would like to thank the following for their help in compiling Gamer's Edition 2020:

2K Games (Gemma Woolnough, Kayleigh Watson); Activision Blizzard (Jonathan Fargher, Emily Woolliscroft, Maxim Samoylenko, Steven Khoo, Kevin Scarpati, Dustin Blackwell, Greg Robyn Mukai Koshi, Jacob Nahin, Michaël Quilunn); MTN Event Staffing; Bandai Namco (Lee Kirton); Bethesda (Mark Robins, Steve Merrett); Beverley Williams – Production Suite; Jordan Booth; Capcom (Laura Skelly, Matthew Edwards, Tim Turi, Tristan Corbett, Stefano Barolo); Capybara Games (Matt Repetski); CCP Games (Paul Elsy, George Kelion, Klaus Wichmand); CD Projekt Red (Robert Malinowski, Radek Adam Grabowski); Sami Çetin; Chucklefish (Molly Carroll, Eric Barone, Tom Katkus); Clifford French (Zakir Hasan); Cloud Imperium Games (David Swofford, Chris Roberts); D'Avekki Studios (Tim Cowles); Daybreak Game Company (Raquel Marcelo); Dead Good Media (Stu Taylor, Matthew Pellett); Double Fine Productions (James Spafford); Edelman (Jules Delay); Electronic Arts (Bryony Gittins, Adam Hay); Epic Games (Julia); ESL (Anna Rozwandowicz, Chrystina Martel, Christopher Flato); Esportsearnings; Evolve PR (Albertine Watson, Shawn Petraschuk, Tom Ohle); Forty Seven (Dillon Arace); Freejam Games (Martin Snelling, Andy Griffiths); Frontier Developments (Daniela Pietrosanu); Gameloft (Jack Wilcock); GameRankings; Global Game Jam (Seven Siegel, Gorm Lai, Jo Summers); GosuGamers (Victor Martyn, Ed Harmer); Grayling (Sam Gavin); H+K Strategies (George Cullen, Maddie Richards, Priya Sund, Kandace Williamson); Hakoom (aka A-Hakam A-Karim); Headup Games (Gregor Ebert); Hope & Glory PR (Sheeraz Gulsher, Pieter Graham); Housemarque (Lauri Immonen); id Software (Tim Willits); Image & Form (Brjann Sigurgeirsson); Indigo Pearl (Caroline Miller, Alex Holt-Kulapalan, Robbie Paterson, Luke Bennett; Anita Wong; Iga Kowacka); IO Interactive (Jeppe Kåre Sørensen, Travis Barbour, Theuns Smit, Clemens E Koch) Jelly Media (Mark Bamber); Johnny Atom Productions (Simon Callaghan); Koch Media (Daniel Emery, Joshua Ball); Laminar Research (Marty Arant);

Andrew Laughlin; Lick PR (Kat Osman, Lucy Starvis, Ryan Sinclair); Limited Run Games (Josh Fairhurst, Douglas Bogart); Charles Martinet; MCV (Seth Barton, Marie Dealessandri); Microsoft (Kumar Manix, Rob Semsey, Rebecca Gordius); Mohn Media (Anke Frosch, Theo Loechter, Marina Rempe, Reinhild Regragui, Jeanette Sio, Dennis Thon, Christin Moeck, Jens Pähler); Mojang; Motion Twin (Benjamin Laulan); Bruce Nash; Nintendo (Emma Danna, Kilwach Tailor, Oliver Coe); NIS America (Chris Olw Prius), Namada Studio; Numantian Games (Miguel Corral); Outrageous PR (Danielle Woodyatt); Overbuff; Premier PR (Will Beckett, Lauren Dillon, Yunus Ibrahim, Tom Copeland); PrettyGreen (Tania Burnham, Robert Jones); PriceCharting (JJ Hendricks); Print Force; PSNProfiles (Matt Reed); Psyonix (Stephanie Thoensen, Joshua Watson); PUBG Corporation (Shane Rho); Red Consultancy (Graham Westrop, Natasha Zialor, Beth Mitchell); Renaissance PR (Stefano Petrullo); Riot Games (Becca Roberts, Jessica Frucht); Roblox (Brian Jaquet); Kieran Robson; Rockstar Games (Craig Gilmore, Hamish Brown, Patricia Pucci); Rocksteady Studios (Gaz Deaves); RockyNoHands (aka Rocky Stoutenburgh); Roll7 (Simon Bennett); Katia Sae; Joseph Saelee; Gianluca Schappei; Sega (Peter Oliver); Shoryuken; SonicFox (Dominique McLean); Sony Interactive Entertainment (Sarah Moffatt, Jess Benson, Aaron Kaufman); Speedrun (Peter Chase); Sports Interactive (Ciaran Brennan, Neil Brock, Miles Jacobson); Spotify (Martin Vacher); Square Enix (Ian Dickson); SRK FGC Stats (@SRKRanking); Stallion83 (aka Raymond Cox); Stature PR; StudioMDHR (Ryan Moldenhauer, Chad Moldenhauer); SuperData (Sam Barberie, Albert Ngo); SwipeRight PR (Kirsty Endfield); (Jennie Kong); Team Plant (Victoria Britton, Henry Eric Plant, Inky, Bruce); thatgamecompany; Think Jam (Ellie Graham, Chris White); THQ Nordic; TrueAchievements (Rich Stone); TT Games; Jack Turner; Twitch (Chase); Ubisoft (Stefan McGarry, David Burroughs, Adam Merrett, Olivia Garner, Katie Laurence, Calum Ridgewell); VGChartz (Craig Snow); Warner Bros. (Mark Ward, Hannah Jacob, Bethany Hearn); XG Group; YouTube Gaming (George Panayotopoulos); ZaziNombies (aka Kyle L Neville); Zebra Partners (Beth Llewelyn).

Code	Country	Code	Country	Code	Country
ABW	Aruba	GMB	Gambia		
AFG	Afghanistan	GNB	Guinea-Bissau		
AGO	Angola	GNQ	Equatorial		
AIA	Anguilla		Guinea	PLW	Palau
ALB	Albania	GRC	Greece	PNG	Papua New Guinea
AND	Andorra	GRD	Grenada	POL	Poland
ANT	Netherlands	GRL	Greenland	PRI	Puerto Rico
	Antilles	GTM	Guatemala	PRK	Korea, DPRO
ARG	Argentina	GUF	French Guiana	PRT	Portugal
ARM	Armenia	GUM	Guam	PRY	Paraguay
ASM	American Samoa	GUY	Guyana	PYF	French Polynesia
ATA	Antarctica	HKG	Hong Kong	QAT	Qatar
ATF	French Southern	HMD	Heard and	REU	Réunion
	Territories		McDonald Islands	ROM	Romania
ATG	Antigua and	HND	Honduras	RUS	Russian Federation
	Barbuda	HRV	Croatia (Hrvatska)	RWA	Rwanda
AUS	Australia	HTI	Haiti	SAU	Saudi Arabia
AUT	Austria	HUN	Hungary	SDN	Sudan
AZE	Azerbaijan	IDN	Indonesia	SEN	Senegal
BDI	Burundi	IND	India	SGP	Singapore
BEL	Belgium	IOT	British Indian	SGS	South Georgia and
BEN	Benin		Ocean Territory		South SS
BFA	Burkina Faso	IRL	Ireland	SHN	Saint Helena
BGD	Bangladesh	IRN	Iran	SJM	Svalbard and
BGR	Bulgaria	IRQ	Iraq		Jan Mayen
BHR	Bahrain	ISL	Iceland		Islands
BHS	The Bahamas	ISR	Israel	SLB	Solomon Islands
BIH	Bosnia and	ITA	Italy	SLE	Sierra Leone
	Herzegovina	JAM	Jamaica	SLV	El Salvador
BLR	Belarus	JOR	Jordan	SMR	San Marino
BLZ	Belize	JPN	Japan	SOM	Somalia
BMU	Bermuda	KAZ	Kazakhstan	SPM	Saint Pierre and
BOL	Bolivia	KEN	Kenya		Miquelon
BRA	Brazil	KGZ	Kyrgyzstan	SRB	Serbia
BRB	Barbados	KHM	Cambodia	SSD	South Sudan
BRN	Brunei Darussalam	KIR	Kiribati	STP	São Tomé and
BTN	Bhutan	KNA	Saint Kitts and		Príncipe
BVT	Bouvet Island		Nevis	SUR	Suriname
BWA	Botswana	KOR	Korea, Republic of	SVK	Slovakia
CAF	Central African	KWT	Kuwait	SVN	Slovenia
	Republic	LAO	Laos	SWE	Sweden
CAN	Canada	LBN	Lebanon	SWZ	Swaziland
CCK	Cocos (Keeling)	LBR	Liberia	SYC	Seychelles
	Islands	LBY	Libya	SYR	Syrian Arab
CHE	Switzerland	LCA	Saint Lucia		Republic
CHL	Chile	LIE	Liechtenstein	TCA	Turks and Caicos
CHN	China	LKA	Sri Lanka		Islands
CIV	Côte d'Ivoire	LSO	Lesotho	TCD	Chad
CMR	Cameroon	LTU	Lithuania	TGO	Togo
COD	Congo, DR of the	LUX	Luxembourg	THA	Thailand
COG	Congo	LVA	Latvia	TJK	Tajikistan
COK	Cook Islands	MAC	Macau	TKL	Tokelau
COL	Colombia	MAR	Morocco	TKM	Turkmenistan
COM	Comoros	MCO	Monaco	TMP	East Timor
CPV	Cape Verde	MDA	Moldova	TON	Tonga
CRI	Costa Rica	MDG	Madagascar	TPE	Chinese
CUB	Cuba	MDV	Maldives		Taipei
CXR	Christmas	MEX	Mexico	TTO	Trinidad and
	Island	MHL	Marshall Islands		Tobago
CYM	Cayman Islands	MKD	Macedonia	TUN	Tunisia
CYP	Cyprus	MLI	Mali	TUR	Turkey
CZE	Czech Republic	MLT	Malta	TUV	Tuvalu
DEU	Germany	MMR	Myanmar (Burma)	TZA	Tanzania
DJI	Djibouti	MNE	Montenegro	UAE	United Arab
DMA	Dominica	MNG	Mongolia		Emirates
DNK	Denmark	MNP	Northern Mariana	UGA	Uganda
DOM	Dominican		Islands	UK	United Kingdom
	Republic	MOZ	Mozambique	UKR	Ukraine
DZA	Algeria	MRT	Mauritania	UMI	US Minor Islands
ECU	Ecuador	MSR	Montserrat	URY	Uruguay
EGY	Egypt	MTQ	Martinique	USA	United States of
ERI	Eritrea	MUS	Mauritius		America
ESH	Western Sahara	MWI	Malawi	UZB	Uzbekistan
ESP	Spain	MYS	Malaysia	VAT	Holy See
EST	Estonia	MYT	Mayotte		(Vatican City)
ETH	Ethiopia	NAM	Namibia	VCT	Saint Vincent
FIN	Finland	NCL	New Caledonia		and the
FJI	Fiji	NER	Niger		Grenadines
FLK	Falkland Islands	NFK	Norfolk Island	VEN	Venezuela
	(Malvinas)	NGA	Nigeria	VGB	Virgin Islands
FRA	France	NIC	Nicaragua		(British)
FRG	West Germany	NIU	Niue	VIR	Virgin Islands (US)
FRO	Faroe Islands	NLD	Netherlands	VNM	Vietnam
FSM	Micronesia,	NOR	Norway	VUT	Vanuatu
	Federated	NPL	Nepal	WLF	Wallis and Futuna
	States of	NRU	Nauru		Islands
FXX	France,	NZ	New Zealand	WSM	Samoa
	Metropolitan	OMN	Oman	YEM	Yemen
GAB	Gabon	PAK	Pakistan	ZAF	South Africa
GEO	Georgia	PAN	Panama	ZMB	Zambia
GHA	Ghana	PCN	Pitcairn	ZWE	Zimbabwe
GIB	Gibraltar		Islands		
GIN	Guinea	PER	Peru		
GLP	Guadeloupe	PHL	Philippines		

STOP PRESS!

Just as certain as the Sun rising in the morning – or Mario defeating Bowser – is the fact that gaming records keep on being broken. Here, we've amassed a bonanza of records that were set just as we were going to press…

First person to earn every *Sea of Thieves* achievement

Microsoft's pirate-'em-up *Sea of Thieves* (2018) has a notoriously difficult list of achievements. It took Xbox gamer "Zyx" around 2,000 hours to unlock all 60 of them! He completed the feat on 17 Nov 2018, saying that the "Merchant Forager" achievement was the "most gruelling" of all.

First no-hit completion of the "Soulsborne" series

On 20 Mar 2019, Twitch streamer "The Happy Hob" (UK) completed what he had dubbed "The God Run" – a no-hit completion of all five FromSoftware-developed "Soulsborne" games. He took them on in the order *Bloodborne* (2015), *Dark Souls II* (2014), *Dark Souls* (2011), *Demon's Souls* (2009) and *Dark Souls III* (2016) and emerged without suffering so much as a scratch!

Fastest completion of *Sekiro*

The average play-through of *Sekiro: Shadows Die Twice* (Activision, 2019) takes around 25 hours. Yet "Mazirika" (CHN) took just 22 min 41 sec to cut a path through the absurdly difficult ninja game. Speedrun verified the PC gamer's time on 2 May 2019.

Highest-grossing movie inspired by videogaming

As of 26 Apr 2019, *Ready Player One* (USA, 2018) had taken $579,290,136 (£449,146,000) at the worldwide box office. The Steven Spielberg–directed movie is largely set within a game-like virtual-reality world called the OASIS and features well-known characters from various games.

Fastest marathon dressed as a games character (female)

On 28 Apr 2019 at the 39th annual London Marathon in the UK, Shaolin Loke (UK) achieved the fastest marathon dressed as a games character. She completed the race in 3 hr 56 min 18 sec while wearing an outfit inspired by *Street Fighter*'s Chun-Li. Her costume included Chun-Li's iconic blue qipao dress and her spiked wrist bracelets.

Highest Xbox Live GamerScore

Stand aside "Stallion83" (see pp.70–71) because "smrnov" (aka Stephen Rowe, CAN) is the new leader in the GamerScore stakes. As of 26 Apr 2019, he had 2,162,420 points – over 100,000 more than the USA's "Stallion83".

Largest collection of *God of War* memorabilia

Emmanuel Mojica Rosas's collection of *God of War*-inspired memorabilia consists of 570 items and was verified in Xalisco, Nayarit, Mexico, on 3 Mar 2019. The Mexican's haul includes items from across Sony Interactive Entertainment's Santa Monica Studio franchise. Emmanuel even has the gold master-copy disc of *God of War* (2018), which was presented to him by Game Director Cory Barlog.

Most tweeted-about game (current)

Though it didn't release actual figures, Twitter did confirm in a blog post on 22 Jan 2019 that *Fate/Grand Order* (Aniplex, 2015) was the most tweeted-about game in 2018. The free-to-play RPG for Android and iOS devices is particularly popular in Japan, where it's become something of a phenomenon – so much so that even Epic's *Fortnite* had to settle for second place in Twitter's top 10!

The game is a tactical, turn-based RPG in which players summon "Servants" that they direct in battle.

Most playable characters in a hack-and-slash game

Warriors Orochi 4 (2018), developed and published by Koei Tecmo Games (JPN), has a roster of 170 playable fighters (you can see just a small portion of them above). As of 26 Apr 2019, the mash-up between *Dynasty Warriors* and *Samurai Warriors* (both Koei Tecmo) continues to be the hack-and-slash game with the most characters.

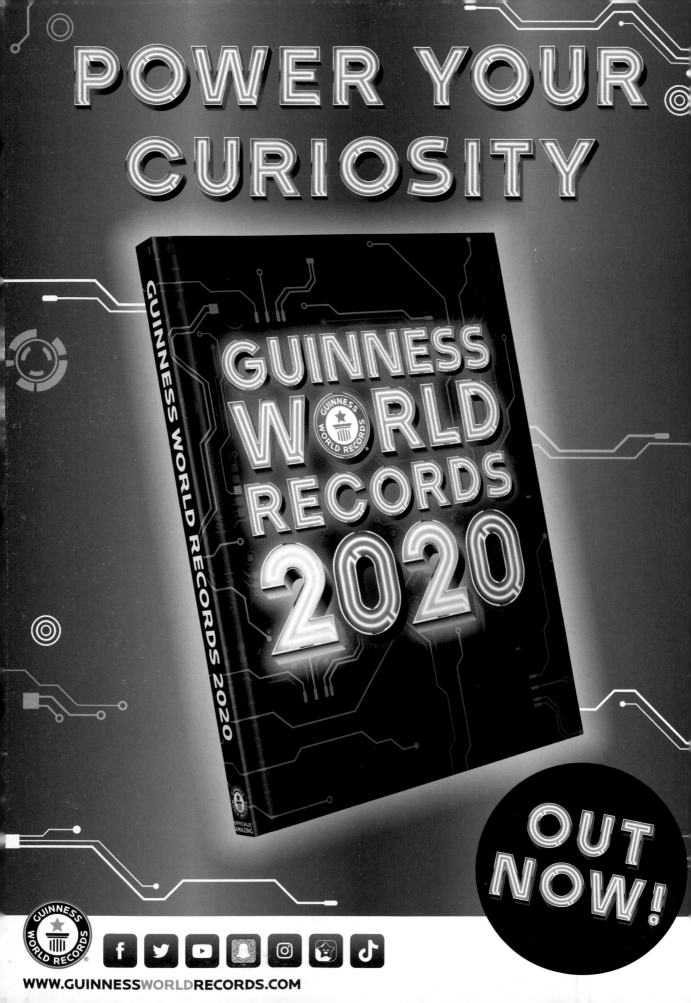

POWER YOUR CURIOSITY

GUINNESS WORLD RECORDS 2020

OUT NOW!

WWW.GUINNESSWORLDRECORDS.COM